I Broke The Code, SO CAN You!

R. Ivan Turner

Table of Contents

In Dedication

To my loving mother, Fay, my guardian angel sister, Kimberly, my exceedingly intelligent brother, Timothy, each of who were contributors to my success, and my beautiful daughters, Ivana and Sara. I would be remiss if I failed to mention Debra Jean Hunt and so many others who have been a source of healing in my arduous period of recovery during the past two years following a life-threatening head injury.

Each of you are my inspiration. Thanks for your love, warmth, support, and the countless years of laughter and togetherness!

To my dear friends throughout the restoration industry, insurance industry, world of academia and the entrepreneurial world. It is with your help that I am able to write this manuscript. While it would be impossible to list each one of my friends, I will rest in knowing that you know who you are. Your presence in my life has had immeasurable and lasting rewards.

Finally, a special word of acknowledgment for my former business partner and the many dedicated, hardworking and giving employees that I had the distinct pleasure of working with through the years. While you may not have always been highly recognized in the call of duty under my charge, know that you were valued, and will always hold a special place in my heart. It is with my deepest love that I pray for your utmost success, health and peace through your journey in life.

To my Heavenly Father. You loved the world so much that you gave your only son, for whosoever believeth in you shall not perish, but have everlasting life.

God I thank you this day for the thoughts in my mind, strength of my body, calmness of my heart, and the steady guidance of my hand, as I wrote the words for which I had never heard.

Faithfully Yours,
Ivan

Foreword

I was first introduced to Ivan Turner and Show Me Marketing in the Spring of 2013. For the prior five years, I had been given the opportunity to coach and mentor some of the top leaders and coaches in the "In Home Services" industry, specifically the Carpet Cleaning, Restoration and Rug Washing venues. My background included being the Chief Negotiator for Michael Gerber, author and founder of Emyth Worldwide, a Founding Partner with the John Maxwell Group, worked with Howard Partridge and Phenomenal Products and spent time as President of a national ATM company. During that time I was on the board of the International Franchise Association's Educational Foundation, National Co-Vice Chair of the National Federation of Independent Business Foundation and have been called "the Coaches Coach". I had found that some of the most authentic and hardworking individuals make up the in home services industry and for the most part they treat their clients, employees and prospects with honesty, integrity, dignity and respect. In other words, they go above and beyond to produce the results that the homeowners want and expect. One afternoon I received an email from Ivan Turner inquiring about my coaching and mentoring services. Before I contacted Ivan I did my homework and research. I found out through my contacts in the industry that Ivan Turner was not only a true gentleman but that he had created a major company in the Restoration industry. Upon further due diligence I found out that Ivan's value system was focused upon making a difference for his clients, staff and his community. Ivan had my complete attention and I wanted to find out if the word on the street was true.

It took about 15 minutes into our conversation when I pleasantly discovered that Ivan Turner does walk his talk. His mission and passion at this point in his successful career was to become the leading teacher, coach and authority to assist in easing the burden of the hardworking restoration and cleaning business owners. Ivan claimed that he UNLOCKED THE CODE to not only financial success but also to living a successful life. The tools, the observations and the processes in this book will span almost any entrepreneurial endeavor. All businesses are the same in that they need to become better than good in the lead generation, lead conversion and client fulfillment processes inside of their business.

During one of our initial conversations, I suggested to Ivan that he should write a book to reach a larger audience than just his coaching clients. Of course, we all have a book inside of us but not everyone will rise to the occasion to put their thoughts, hopes, dreams, aspirations and information down for others to read. The writing of a book takes courage, commitment, passion and perseverance more than you can imagine. It was in that conversation that Ivan said he always wanted to tell his story since whatever the mind of man can conceive and believe, it can achieve. The very proof is in your hands; *I Broke the Code* is a reality. The reader will learn never been told before secrets, systems and procedures that they will not find anywhere else. Ivan KNOWS what he is writing about. Ivan lived, failed, attempted, succeeded and now wants to teach you how *I Broke the Code* to owning and managing uber successful business that will allow you to really live a life worth living. A life filled with prosperity and fulfillment, giving you the time, resources and energy to really make a difference in this world.

Read, take notes, prove, attempt, do the work, set your goals, track your results, adjust and keep moving forward. As one of my most respected clients and friends, Howard Partridge states the reason most businesses are not successful is all because of FTI. Yes, Failure to Implement—to do the work, is the major reason why most small companies do not receive the benefits of their hard work. Read this book, follow Ivan's advice, do the required work, monitor the results, set higher goals, and just DO IT!

Sincerely,
Mark Ehrlich

Introduction

F amily and friends have asked why I decided to write this book. The answer is surprisingly simple. I have had the good fortune of having been the beneficiary of knowledge, advice, support—and most importantly—encouragement along the way through acts of kindness from generous colleagues, friends, and even strangers. On the higher level of giving, I want to share information and encouragement to those involved in the cleaning and restoration industry and all entrepreneurs. Though we may speak our own unique vernacular, we share the universal spirit of entrepreneurship with all those in business across all service and product lines.

I think you will agree that this is more than a business book or a how-to book on starting and succeeding in your business, although there is plenty of that advice included! No, this book is more about hope, dreams, and how you, too, can make a difference.

Throughout the pages you will discover tried and true advice on how to operate your business, succeed as a restoration expert, and more. However, my hope is you will realize the more important role you play. To work hard, keep grounded, dream big, and always give back.

I want to encourage others through my successes and failures. Throughout the pages, you will get the opportunity to learn from both. By learning how it's done from someone who has lived it and has been in business for over 25 years, you will be able to discover how you, too, can succeed.

You see, for me I can remember every fire, every flood, and I can clearly see every person I have met through the years. No, I cannot remember all their names, but I do remember their faces and their emotionally charged feelings. I also remember how we were able to turn things around for them at a time they needed it most. This is the hope that you can give families as you restore their faith, their homes, and do all you can to give their lives back to them. The hope that tomorrow will be a new day, a better day.

The life of a restorer is not an easy one. In fact, it can be quite tough at times. Can you imagine daily witnessing families torn apart and facing the worst times of their lives? Whether they have lost their homes to a fire or a tornado, or experienced floods and the devastation that results from that, it is hard. Think about how difficult it is to walk in a home where someone has just experienced that and the helplessness they feel. I know at times I walked into the unforgettable pungent odor-filled environment and could still see the residual fire particles wafting through the air, see the smoke on their faces, watch as their tears were flowing, and knew that their road ahead would be a difficult one, at least for now.

And that is where you come in. You alone can be their strength and support. You get to show them that there will be a tomorrow and you will do everything possible to turn it around and restore their lives and property again.

For me, this was perhaps my strongest suit. I also possessed an innate ability to convey my empathy. When I was with a family that was weeping after losing their home, I showed them how rewarding it would be when we got it back up and running again. We often can't replace those lost treasures or photo albums, but we can take what is left and get the most out of it. At a time like this, the little things often matter the most.

I believe I discovered my life's purpose one Christmas Eve while responding to a house fire. The husband had accidentally set his house on fire while cooking breakfast for his wife of forty plus years. Now we respond to many fires, especially during the holidays, but what made this one stand out was the fact that one year to the day that family had lost their daughter in a tragic auto accident. They were absolutely devastated. They could not have cared less about the rest of the home, but what was most important to the family was to restore their daughter's bedroom. That room had gone untouched since her tragic accident. The stuffed animals and all her personal possessions were extremely important to them. I knew then how important my role was. I was able to successfully help them and countless others before and after that. When the project finally ended, we stood together in the newly remodeled kitchen and embraced in tearful hugs before my departure. There were no scheduled victory celebrations or hoopla. My part was over, I had restored another life.

The strength of the human spirit is incredible and we get to witness that over and over again. We work with families to show them it will get better. We will get them back to where they were before.

This book will detail my best practices and the knowledge I have picked up through the hundreds of fire damage jobs, thousands of floods, and about every other natural and man-made calamity you can image.

I started my journey with very little money, in an efficiency apartment with no family background or business expertise. I grew the business through a lot of hard work, dedication, a little luck and determination. Today the business continues to flourish under new ownership.

Throughout the years, my determination to succeed, as well as continually attending dozens of classes and a thirst for always learning more, helped prepare me for the challenges I encountered. I also learned from all my mistakes. It often felt like an up and down roller coaster. But it is truly the best thing I have ever experienced—except the birth of my daughters, of course.

But it is important to note, I didn't become an entrepreneur to make a lot of money. That was secondary. My mother brought us up with good values and ethics. I was taught if you work hard and believe, you can achieve anything you set your mind to. I truly believe you will get paid back ten-fold. It is the law of reciprocity—the more you give, the more you get back. The money will follow, and follow me it did. I recommend you don't place money above people ever. We were brought up this way. And I hope you too, after reading this, will want to do the same.

The book shows what works and what doesn't work. It will guide you to be a great entrepreneur because you will have the knowledge to succeed. It will also be the encouragement you need to succeed and face those challenges. As an entrepreneur, you take risks, you work long, hard hours that can take time away from family, sometimes 16 to 18 hours a day. You have the right to grow your business and only the entrepreneur can decide what success means to him or her. No one can take that away from you. Times can be tough and a lot of entrepreneurs become defeated. They give up too soon and give up on the entrepreneurial spirit. Know that you aren't alone. Entrepreneurs are a like family and will help each other. There truly is nothing better.

Being in business also affords you the opportunity to spend time with your family and to show them how dreams are possible. My children are my life and this book is my legacy to them. I have two beautiful daughters— Ivana and Sara Fay. Sara was diagnosed with brain cancer at a very young age. She had 13 tumors on her spine and was not expected to live past the age of five. But Sara is a survivor and her perseverance always shines through. She has gone through brain surgery, chemotherapy, radiation, spinal surgery, and more. It's a true testament to the human spirit. Today at 17 she continues to grow, and we couldn't be prouder.

Her sister, Ivana, is 20 years old. It has been painful for her to see her sister go through the trials and tribulations and the constant fear that her little sister wouldn't make it. However, she never wavered and was determined to be the strength we all needed. She demonstrated that best as a friend and a guardian angel for her little sister. As a parent I couldn't ask for any more.

That is one of the reasons why much of the proceeds of this book will go to St. Jude Hospital. It is my way to show that we can make a difference. I encourage you to do the same. Together we can contribute to the fight against this scourge and one day, break the code of curing Cancer. Never stop giving. Always give back and your life and business will be blessed beyond belief.

This isn't the life I had envisioned for myself. Growing up, I thought I would be a Navy fighter pilot and transition into a commercial airline career. Well, I did join the Navy at 17, though my fighter pilot dreams and aspirations eluded me. I did receive my pilot's license at the age of eighteen and found fulfillment in the realm of general aviation. On the U.S.S. Tripoli, I traveled all over the Western Pacific and had some of the best days of my life. During midnight watches on the ship's bridge, I would contemplate my future while watching the stars. At times, the sea was as smooth as glass and the stars shone as brilliant as sparkling diamonds. You could almost reach out and touch them. I realized my journey in life was going to be special. I determined early on to define my purpose. Even today, when I face challenges, and there are many, I will go back to that special time and re-live those nights gazing at the stars. I then can reclaim my peace and serenity and deal with the problems at hand.

You never know when the next storm or disaster will strike, but you can be the calm in the storm and help those families get their lives back together.

As Henry David Thoreau wrote, "Most men lead lives of quiet desperation and go to the grave with the song still in them." I understand that. Take me to other places I will never go. We all have a story to tell and this is my story, this is my song. I hope you enjoy it and make your journey a successful and prosperous one.

The Pen is Mightier than the Sword

I t has been said that the pen is mightier than the sword. With its every deliberate stroke, those who wield it have in their power the ability to weaken the will of the strongest of men, or strengthen the will of the weakest of men.

Throughout the ages, the pen has been used destructively to convey hatred. It has spelled out the articles of war, pitting one nation and its people against another, though separated by vast bodies of water. Even in this wonderful place where we all live, it is imprudently used to obliterate and disparage others, who perhaps hold a conflicting point of view.

It has been used to spread love and form a kinship with complete strangers since the beginning of time. Some of its simplest renderings as I love you, please forgive me, thank you, or, you are a very special person, have forever changed the lives of its recipients.

The quill and ink well have since been replaced with the electronic keyboard, allowing for the message of the purveyor of love and hate to travel at the speed of sound. Today my pen is guided by energy much greater than that of the mind.

My feelings emanate from the deepest recess of my soul, as I share this story of inspiration and love that will undoubtedly be in this world long past the life of its humble author.

One Saturday I made a trek to St. Louis to check on two employees who had been attending a three-day advanced drying class. It wasn't unusual for me to stop in on training classes to offer moral support to my employees.

The purpose of this visit was two-fold: to offer that moral support, in addition to an eagerly anticipated dinner with the instructor, Barry Costa.

Every teacher has his or her unique way of edifying his course work. Some lean heavily on written matter, while others focus more on sharing their own life experiences to allow the student a broader understanding of the challenges that they will face.

Barry was different, much different.

He tenderly guided his students through the subject of water restoration as if he were a loving father passing on his craft to his children.

It was truly amazing to see the radiance in the eyes of his attentive pupils as he gently shaped their malleable minds like a potter shapes his clay into a great work of art.

Before this day, I had never formally met Barry. I had seen him at many industry events scampering about, helping others but had always been too busy to stop and properly introduce myself.

Many know that Barry and his wife lost their beautiful daughter, Kimberly, to a form of cancer at the young age of 19. It is this appalling disease that inexorably unites the Costa's to so many other families that have been afflicted with this disease, my own included.

During dinner, we laughed together and discussed and shared our thoughts on a variety of subjects. We immediately recognized that we share many commonalities aside from our experience with cancer.

As I sat listening to Barry, it was palpable to me that the spirit of Kim lives and shines vibrantly through her loving father.

My quiet drive back to my home in Jefferson City on this evening was different from the countless times I have traveled this familiar artery. The frigid night sky was murky with an overcast of clouds.

My heart was overflowing with a light that was burning bright, as I contemplated many of life's questions.

I have often questioned why God would allow his precious children to suffer from disease and hardship. The answer up until now has always been as fleeting as the answer to the age-old question of the purpose of life.

Each spring marks the seasonal rebirth of mother earth. The snows begin to melt and the grasses begin to sprout up out of the earth. The trees with their limbs stretched towards the heavens begin to show life as the once young buds now flower into beautiful leaves, each uniquely different from the next.

In celebration of this rebirth, God favors us with the music made by the songbirds that fill the trees with their sound of new life. Like the songbirds, Gods special angels are the messengers that fill our hearts with songs of hope, love, peace and the importance of making a difference in the lives of others who are hurting.

The flesh may succumb to age and disease, but the spirit can never die, as it is born to touch the lives of others for the ages to follow. Though I had never met Kim in person, I learned more from her on this evening than I have from others that I have known for my entire life.

Her benevolent spirit touched me on this evening as if I were touched by an angel. Thank you Kimberly Costa, for making a difference in my life and in the lives of untold others.

Your song of hope and love will echo throughout the ages.

To the Costa family, thank you for generously sharing Kim's love and passion for life. You are blessed.

In closing, let today mark the rebirth of your life. Live life passionately and touch the lives of others!

Welcome

The intention of this book is to offer you all of the information, documents, best practices and thought processes that you will need to consider prior to starting your own cleaning and restoration business. The arena of disaster restoration is a decidedly competitive one, and you will need to have all of your 'ducks in a row' before you get started, in order to hit the ground running and have success right from the start. Far from a get-rich-quick business, working in restoration requires consistent effort and continuous innovation to stay ahead of the competition and wind up with a business that is profitable in the long term. Is it going to be a lot of hard work with many ups and downs along the way? Yes—it very likely will be. Is it going to be worth it in the end? If you work hard and stay focused on your goals, it will be more than worth all your pains when all is said and done.

The organization of this book is intentional as it will lead you through everything that you need to know in order to enter and excel in this rewarding industry. We will start out by learning more about the restoration industry itself and what is going to be required of you in order to succeed. Some of the most central points during the first sections of the book include deciding whether to open a franchise or go it alone, what some of the most important trends are within the industry, and who some of the major players are within the market currently.

From there we will transition into the actual running of the business itself. This section includes an interesting look at different personality types that are drawn to working within this business and the strengths and weaknesses that each bring to the job. It would be wise to take some time thinking about these profiles and how they relate to you. There is a chance that one of them will fit you perfectly, or perhaps you are more of a blend of various 'characters'. With a good understanding of what you are bringing to the table in terms of the business operation, you will be better prepared to hire the right people around you to compliment your skills.

The nuts and bolts of any business, regardless of the industry, are the human resources and accounting departments. Without good people in these areas, or managing them properly yourself, your business will flounder even if there are plenty of customers to go around. This book will provide you with both advice and documentation to get your HR and accounting functions off to a great start. HR is important because it will often be the interface between yourself (and other managers) and the employees themselves. With satisfied and well-informed employees, you will have a better chance to meet your business goals. The importance of a good accounting system should speak for itself. With accurate records and current information, decision making is easier and you will have a better chance of guiding the business wisely into the future.

With all of the administration behind us, the book moves on to marketing and sales and how you can attract the customers that are essential to your success. The restoration business relies heavily on other industries for business referrals, such as insurance agents and plumbers, so much of the marketing discussion will center on how to find work from within those groups. Once you get the rudimentary knowledge of how you should be marketing your restoration business, it will be up to you to persistently think of new, cost-effective concepts to pursue. Marketing in this business is a never-ending battle that you can't afford to sleep on even for one day. There is always competition skulking, even for the most successful businesses, so remain aggressive in your marketing efforts from day one onward.

It is my sincere hope that when you are finished with this book, you will feel confident that you have the necessary skill set and information to start or transform an existing, nonetheless average business into a revered powerhouse! In many ways, working in the restoration field is just like running any other business. You must manage costs and people effectively while marketing to the right people in order to see revenues rise while expenses stay in check. However, there are some parts of this business that are unique and you will need to understand that before getting started. This book is aimed at preparing you for all of it, and I feel that I have attained that goal. Enjoy learning about this industry from the following pages, and best of luck in your upcoming endeavors.

Signed,

R. Ivan Turner

Overview

In this book we will discuss many of the aspects that are involved in the day-to-day administrative side of a cleaning and restoration business. It is important to note that every business will operate differently from the next. However, all businesses share common needs such as accounts payable, accounts receivable, collection methods, employee management, marketing and sales, etc. These are all areas of a business that are critical to the business's longevity and success.

You will learn the way that my own service company had operated and continues to operate the administrative arm of the business. After reading and studying the book you should have an impression of the importance of implementing sound procedures into your own business.

Your Administrative Manual is a living document. You must make periodic changes to its contents as your business needs change. One of the most commonly found deficiencies in the average cleaning and restoration business is a poorly run administrative side of the business. Many owners who tend to be excellent on the technical and operations side, may not be so excellent when it comes to the administration needs of a busy service company. The best way to overcome this deficiency, in my opinion, is to hire an individual to write and implement the administrative side of your business. Once the administrative systems are in place in your business, it is you, the owner, who must convey the importance of following these systems with all employees of the company.

In this book I will share a few personal stories that not only cost us a lot of money but, just as importantly, cost us a considerable amount of time that could have been spent growing the business. I'd like to be able to say that we have always been a smooth running operation. However, I would be lying. The truth is that our business like others has had its share of losing money through the years that perhaps may have been avoided. Hopefully you will not make many of the same mistakes that I made.

I have attended dozens of classes through the years that touched on the subject of the financial and administrative side of business. I remember one particular industry class where the speaker paced back and forth across the stage preaching and waving his arms, looking like a Jimmy Swaggert protégé. He gave the hell and brimstone oration of how some business owners in the audience were destined to fail. It still makes the hair on the back of my neck stand up when I painfully recall his sermon. I just knew that this televangelist type of expert was speaking directly to me.

During the sermon, I kept swearing to the good Lord that if he would let my business survive for just a few more months I would change my wicked ways!

Well, as it turned out, I returned home and once again resorted to my wicked ways. The business was steadily flowing in, and I once again took a careless approach to the administrative needs of the business.

My chief and costliest sin was in failing to develop and implement a contracting process for all work that the business would perform. All this on the heels of being forewarned by the preacher that failure to obey the laws of business would in the long run cause me to be cast out of the business community.

In the restoration industry, and even the carpet cleaning industry, getting paid for your services often ends up like being a game of cat and mouse. In this game you have two sides:

Side one is the customer who received the services, and on the opposing side, you have the service provider.

In a perfect world you have a quality service that was delivered with little to no problems and collecting payment for the services is swift and event free. The cleaning and restoration world isn't always this perfect. Ask any experienced restorer about the pitfalls that are associated with the day of payment and you'll hear some stories that for many are enough to be cause for not getting into the business. Sometimes when it's time to collect for restoration services, uncanny personalities of the customer begin to manifest and now the customer who, up until payday, was in love with your services takes on a completely different character, especially when insurance money is involved.

We'll discuss this phenomenon in much more detail in a bit, but for now let me make this one point that you must be mindful of, even when dealing with exceptional customers. **Never, under any circumstances, surrender or lose your leverage.** Your leverage is the written contract between you and the person whom you provided the services to. The vast majority of customers, insured or uninsured, are very happy and eager to pay for work that your company rendered. Just be cognizant of the latent motives from the small percentage of unscrupulous customers as the project nears completion where the customer has seen, or currently holds the tightly clutched insurance draft in their hands.

By now you should have a general idea of the importance of producing and then implementing a set of procedures and systems to address the administrative needs of your business.

In this book you will find many of the systems and procedures that, if implemented, will save you time, work, and best of all will ensure that you continue to receive what is the life blood of all business—money!

Today's Carpet Cleaning Industry

Today there are over 30,000 firms listed as carpet cleaning providers. Out of this group the majority of revenues are derived from the residential sector. The carpet cleaning industry is broken into the following categories:

- Full time carpet cleaning firms—the majority of full time firms appear to specialize in either residential or commercial service. Many offer both services, but due to vast differences between the two operational requirements it appears that specialization in one or the other is the norm.

Residential cleaning involves the cleaning of homes, apartments and other dwellings that can typically be cleaned during normal working hours of 8 a.m.-5 p.m., Monday through Saturday. Homes or apartments that have been vacated and scheduled to be cleaned, are often times done after normal business hours, to maximize the amount of jobs that can be scheduled for the day.

Commercial cleaning typically involves the cleaning of offices, restaurants, child care facilities, stores, etc. Firms that service the commercial sector will offer after hours service. Most commercial facilities have their cleaning scheduled for weekends or after store closing. Restaurants are usually scheduled very late in the evening or very early in the morning hours prior to normal opening.

- Part time carpet cleaning firms—the part time operator is typically a firm comprised of one individual who cleans on his time off and in the evenings performing commercial cleaning.

- Janitorial firms—the majority of janitorial firms specialize in commercial cleaning. When a janitorial contract is secured, carpet cleaning for the facilities is typically not contracted out as a separate service but is expected to be a service that is provided as part of the overall contract. Many commercial facilities have on staff personnel that maintain the floor covering.

- Maid services—also provide residential carpet cleaning services. Many maid services market the service to their own customer base and do not necessarily market to the public at large.

A typical residential provider will have a breakout of revenues as follows:

80% Residential

10% Commercial

10% Upholstery cleaning and loose rug cleaning

The carpet cleaning industry is inundated with operators of every size and many different operating styles. The carpet cleaning industry has a relatively low entry cost, therefore it is attractive to a wide range of people.

Within the carpet cleaning sector is the Oriental & Area Rug Cleaning industry. This side of the industry, unlike the carpet cleaning side, typically requires a significant amount of finances, space, expensive equipment and specialized knowledge. The rug cleaning side ranges from the small two-person operation that offers rug cleaning as part of their overall services, to the full time, large scale automated rug cleaning plants with millions of dollars in annual revenues.

FRANCHISE OR INDEPENDENT

One of the very first, and more important decisions you will need to make when starting your business is whether to operate as part of an existing franchise, or forge your own way as an independent business. Let's look closer at the pros and cons of each option to help you determine the right choice for you and your goals.

According to a 1997 Contract Cleaner Statistical Survey in *Cleaning & Maintenance Magazine*, only 14.4% of carpet cleaning operators were part of a franchise group.

A few thoughts on buying into a franchise. From my own perspective, I've found that the vast majority of independent operators in both the carpet cleaning & the restoration industry appear to have a dislike that is almost palpable for competitors who are part of a franchise group. In recent years a handful of Franchisers have formed relationships with some of the larger insurance carriers to handle most of their insurance repair. This, of course, takes work away from the independent restorer and only serves to widen the divide between franchises and independents. My own thought is that the animosity and hate between the independent and the franchises is misdirected. For the real blame should lie with the insurance carriers who propagate the lies to their own insureds for the sole purpose of earning more money for the insurance company. Later in this manual I'll share an idea or two that can be implemented to overcome this major obstacle.

I've never been part of a franchise group for my own personal reasons, but have also never held any animosity towards them. Franchises do work for many individuals. So if you are serious about getting into the business do yourself a favor and at least look into a franchise.

Becoming a Franchisee

The Definition of a Franchise - A form of business organization in which a firm which already has a successful product or service (the franchiser) enters into a continuing contractual relationship with other businesses (franchisees) operating under the franchises trade name and usually with the franchises guidance, in exchange for a fee.

Franchising has never been more popular than it is today. From fast food outlets like McDonald's to carpet cleaning franchises like Stanley Steemer, to restoration franchises like Service Master, the business landscape of America has changed forever. Where else can you pay a fee and within weeks have a turn-key business.

Taking the franchise route to business ownership makes sense for many reasons. With an established franchise you receive in-depth training, ongoing franchise support, and ready-made advertising materials. The very day that you open for business you have instant name recognition that for the independent can take many years to develop. A good franchise is a business system that has been proven to be effective in building business.

Another major advantage of being part of a franchise group is the networking opportunities. You, as the franchisee, have many other franchises to call upon when you are faced with the tough questions.

Competing against franchises is tough for the independent, but certainly not impossible. Even with the power behind franchises the vast majority of the industry wealth is generated by the independently owned operators. This applies to both carpet cleaning and the restoration industry.

Franchise start-ups will run anywhere from $7,500 up to $75,000. Royalties as a percentage of sales will vary from 2-10%. There are many additional start-up costs which range from $14,000 to $45,000. Many franchises will offer a low down payment and offer monthly payments with little to no interest on the balance. The franchises will assist you with advertising ideas, business stationary, business cards, vehicle signs as even with uniform selection.

Some franchises will even lease back equipment and vehicles. The training programs vary from franchise to franchise, but typically offer training programs to include; quality control, comparative cleaning methods, carpet construction and technology, customer service, employee management, motivational ideas, sales tips, and monthly newsletters.

Back to the love/hate relationship between independent and franchises. Believe it or not, even in these supposed times of maturity and civility, it is not all that uncommon to be given the "bird" by a competitor passing you by on the highway. My thought is that it must go along with the competitive nature of the business. You won't find quite the hostility on the restoration side of the industry as you will on the carpet cleaning side, but it is nonetheless still very competitive.

Some of the hostility towards the franchise carpet cleaning companies by the independents stems from what many believe has been decades of false advertising that has hurt not only the independent but the industry as a whole. ChemDry now owned by Home Depot, has been in the cross hairs of the hate for many years. The generalized consensus amongst independents is that their advertising campaign "Squish isn't a sound your carpets should make" implies that having your carpet cleaned by any method besides their Carbonated system will cause mold to grow. Of course, this is, generally speaking, a false statement.

As much as I disagree with their advertising misstatements, and as much as it has appeared to hurt some of their competitors, it is at the end of the day good advertising. It's helped propel the ChemDry brand so far as growth is concerned, and this should be the goal of every business. Build your brand!

The ChemDry website touts itself as "the world's leader for carpet and upholstery cleaning services, cleaning an estimated one billion square feet of carpet each year! What makes ChemDry the world's favorite carpet and upholstery cleaning service is our patented carbonated carpet cleaner, exceptional customer service, and the ongoing research in cleaning technology".

Many independents also have a real dislike for Stanley Steemer. This one I've never quite understood. I suppose it is largely due to envy over the phenomenal success they have enjoyed. Stanley, a very well-run franchise system, has grown to be a very large operation; by far the largest marketer of carpet cleaning services. They are a company that appears to market towards the value minded consumer with their room package specials. An example is three rooms for $99. They advertise heavily in print as well as television and raise the awareness of the need for regularly scheduled cleaning.

There are many reasons for not buying into the franchise concept

Questionable profitability. Most franchisers do not provide much information to potential franchisees regarding earnings possibilities, making it difficult to assess how lucrative investment in the company could be. Even the franchisers who do supply this information usually only give average sales figures and profits before expenses are deducted, numbers that aren't very helpful when trying to determine if your individual franchise will be successful.

Franchising will not likely become a more significant factor in the carpet cleaning industry because a person can obtain all the education they need about the business from the major equipment and chemical suppliers, without having to pay the franchise fee.

High start-up costs. Before opening your franchise, you may be required to pay a non-refundable initial franchise fee, which can cost from several thousand to several hundred thousand dollars. In addition to the initial fee, there are also usually high start-up costs associated with furnishing your franchise with the necessary inventory and equipment. It can easily take several years to recoup the expenses connected with getting your franchise off the ground.

Encroachment. Imagine the following scenario: You have just spent thousands of dollars opening your own cleaning company, when another competitor from the same franchise system opens one within what you believed to be your assigned territory, essentially cutting your customer base in half. This type of thing happens to franchisees all the time, as nearly every franchiser reserves the right to operate anywhere they want.

Lack of legal recourse. As a franchisee, there is little legal recourse that you can take if you are wronged by the franchiser. Most franchisers make franchisees sign agreements waiving his or her rights under applicable federal and state law, and some agreements contain provisions allowing the franchiser to choose the venue and the law under which any dispute would be litigated.

Shamefully, the Federal Trade Commission (FTC), which is supposed to regulate fairness in franchising, investigates less than 6% of the franchise-related complaints it receives.

Limited independence. When you buy a franchise, you are not just buying the right to use the franchiser's name, but you are buying its business plan as well. As a result, most franchisers impose price, appearance, and design standards on franchisees, limiting the ways you can operate the franchise. While these regulations can help promote uniformity, they can also be stifling to franchisees who feel they could run the business more effectively their own way. Often times what ends up happening is that the franchise owner isn't satisfied with the proven systems of the franchiser and starts wanting to "try his own thing". This leads to deep trouble as the franchise agreement has now been breached. Visit any of the cleaning industry bulletin boards and you'll find a few gas bags who were removed from a franchise system whining about the franchisers unfairness.

Royalty payments. Franchisees are generally required to make continuing royalty payments to the franchiser each month based on a percentage of his or her franchise's sales, eating into the franchisee's net profits.

Inflated pricing on supplies. In many cases, the franchiser can designate your franchise's supplier of goods and services. Franchisers argue that this is done to maintain quality control. By not allowing you to shop around and subsequently limiting competition, you are forced to pay higher prices on supplies.

Restrictions on post-term competition. Let's say that you decide to purchase a McDonald's, but after a couple of years you determine that you could run a higher-quality, more profitable burger joint on your own. Unfortunately, due to non-competition clauses built into almost every franchise agreement, franchisees are not allowed to become independent business owners in a similar business after termination of the franchise agreement.

By purchasing a franchise, you may be unwittingly limiting your business opportunities for years after the expiration of your contract. This again causes much grief to the ex-franchise owner who wants to start his own operation without having to pay franchise royalties.

Advertising fees. Many franchisees are obligated to make regular contributions to the franchiser's advertising fund. Franchisers maintain broad discretion over how to administer the advertising fund, and the money you contribute does not necessarily need to be used to target your specific franchise. In a case against Meineke Discount Muffler Shops, for example, it was discovered that Meineke was using the advertising fund for costs totally separate from advertising, yet the case was ruled in Meineke's favor under a verdict that stated that the franchiser has no fiduciary duty to its franchisees!

Unfair termination. Even the slightest impropriety on your part, such as being late on a royalty payment or violating the franchise's standard operating procedure, can be cause for the franchiser to terminate your agreement. While most franchisers are not this strict, the possibility of losing your entire investment for being late on a payment is a scary thought. While these regulations can help promote uniformity, they can also be stifling to franchisees who feel they could run the business more effectively their own way.

I personally know several people who own franchise cleaning and restoration companies. It's amazing how hard some of these folks work to circumnavigate the franchise agreement. What I consider theft, they consider to be looking out for their own best interest. The unscrupulous franchisee will perform cleaning jobs and conveniently forget to report the jobs, whereby not having to pay the agreed upon royalty. On the restoration side of the industry these operators will set up bogus construction companies under names different than that of the franchise so that they are not assessed royalty fees.

After a period of two to three years and the franchise is starting to build momentum, the money starts to flow in regularly and it's at this time when these types of owners begin to feel like they did all the work on their own. Now, with their feathers ruffled and their chest puffed out, they begin to crow like roosters that the franchiser is being overpaid for their services.

Then when they eventually get removed from the system they whine that they were unfairly treated. Anytime there is a group of cleaners together you will inevitably run into one or two gas bags that will give you a hundred good reasons for not buying a franchise.

Major Trends Affecting the Carpet Cleaning Industry

There has been a continual shift the past few years from carpet to hard surfaced flooring. Many homeowners have removed carpeting in their homes in favor of hardwood, ceramic, or the newer laminated flooring products that have become available. This, of course, translates to less carpet to be cleaned by the professional cleaner. By the same token, it opens up new revenue streams for the professional cleaner who becomes trained in cleaning hardwoods, ceramics and other flooring.

Another trend that is advantageous for the professional cleaner is that the consumer has become more concerned and health conscience about the indoor environment. This heightened awareness was brought on by the proliferation of television coverage concerning mold over the past few years, along with a record number of people suffering from allergies.

Dr. Michael Berry wrote a very interesting book titled *The Built Environment*. In his book he addresses indoor air quality issues that are of high value to the carpet-cleaning firm which builds and markets its services to the health conscience consumer.

One of the biggest problems in the cleaning and restoration industry is finding good qualified team members. Make no mistake about it; as much as you might love the field of cleaning, most people of the working age do not consider cleaning to be a career track.

The Business Model

I f you are reading this material you, are either undertaking the planning stages for starting a cleaning and restoration business, or perhaps you are currently in the business and are looking for a way to increase business, while streamlining your operation. Either way we're glad you're here and want to make your journey down the long and winding road to business success a good one.

The multi-billion dollar cleaning and restoration industry is a wonderful and very much needed industry. We restore the lives and property of people who need our help.

The advantages of operating a restoration service are numerous, including:

- A continuing need for services by insurers.
- No inventories to resell; excellent cash flow.
- Industry closing in on the mature cycle.
- Recession resistant business.
- Barriers to start ups.

Trends

Today's entrepreneurs must keep abreast of these sweeping changes, otherwise they will join the legions of rusted, worn out, broken down businesses that lay to the side of the road of entrepreneurship. Quoting Anthony Greenback, author of *The Book of Survival*, "To live through an impossible situation, you don't need the reflexes of a Grand Prix driver, the muscles of a Hercules, the mind of an Einstein. You simply need to know what to do"

I'm here to share with you some of the things you need to do if you are hoping to take your business from average—to a **Powerhouse!**

To make that transition it all begins with thinking like a marketer. Technical prowess doesn't make your phone ring—marketing and sales do.

The five key components to building a successful Cleaning and Restoration Business will include a mix of the following;

1. Understanding how the game is played
2. Great communications
3. Building a great team
4. Developing an innovative game strategy
5. Learning to speak their vernacular

Every journey begins with charting your course and planning for potential obstacles and setbacks along the journey. As an entrepreneur there are various roads which you can take. Each direction will yield diverse outcomes, along with challenges and rewards. I have traveled each of these roads and can tell you with conviction that only one road yielded a substantial difference in my business career. The road to Transformation!

1. You can opt to follow the herd.
2. You can opt to follow the road to the same old same old.
3. You can choose to follow the road to transformation.

Following the herd is perhaps the easiest and safest route that an entrepreneur can follow. You simply do what every other cleaning and restoration operator is doing. After all it is human nature to have a tendency to take the path of least resistance. When you finally do arrive at the trough you will only receive what monetary rewards remain from the herd that preceded your arrival. This is not to mention that you will have to wade through a great deal of manure along the way. Taking this route exemplifies the phrase —monkey see, monkey do!

Following the road of same old same old, may indeed get you to your destination. However this path can be chock full of setbacks, obstacles and one self-induced agonizing defeat after another. When on this route, the entrepreneur has a tendency to be reactionary and continually becomes aggrieved by paralysis through analysis. He makes an attempt at moving forward to achieve something beneficial for his business and it fails. Then he makes another attempt using the same failed process as the first attempt. This futile cycle of using a failed process becomes habitual. Taking this route reminds me of the classic Albert Einstein definition of insanity—Doing the same thing over and over again and expecting a different result.

The One-Trick Pony

"One-trick pony" is a term that can be interpreted a number of ways, depending on who is asked to define it. For some, a one-trick pony might be a musician or band who once topped the billboard charts, but has since all but disappeared from the pop culture scene. A prime example would be Right Said Fred, with his super one-hit wonder "I'm Too Sexy." Apparently, Fred was too sexy for another popular song.

Some reflect back to the age of youth when the traveling three-ring circus swept through town. The promoters and loathsome carnival barkers promised entertainment for all ages: the bearded woman for the curious, the two-headed cow for the twisted, the dancing poodles for the aged, and the one-trick pony for the kids.

Whinnying ponies circled around spotlighted rings with a smattering of applause from the crowd. After a few trips around the ring, the ringmaster would lead the pony to the bright center, and the enthralled children anxiously looked forward to what the pony would do next. At the ringmaster's command, the neatly groomed pony, adorned with ribbons, would bend at the withers and offer a dramatic genuflection for the crowd. The crowd would hoot and cheer, and then the ringmaster would take a lap around the ring, bowing for crowd members on each side of the arena. The pony would patiently await a carrot or sugar cube, and then the ringmaster would load the pony up to move on to the next circus.

Similarly, many cleaning and restoration entrepreneurs promise services in many categories: water damage, carpet cleaning, fire damage, etc. Regardless of how a person interprets the familiar term "one-trick pony," it is not an impressive way to describe something. Too often cleaning and restoration entrepreneurs wear the label of "one-trick pony." Repeatedly they prance around the metaphorical "ring" with a poorly choreographed sales pitch, simply in hopes of being seen and heard by prospective customers, insurance agents, and adjusters, while anxiously awaiting a referral reward. One-trick cleaning and restoration business owners are serious-minded entrepreneurs who struggle to continue the momentum after the success of their one and only triumphant feat has waned.

Fear not, one-trick ponies—it does not have to be that way!

Unfortunately, little ponies are for kids. When entering the high-stakes ring of business, one must do so with the commanding presence of a majestic Lipizzaner stallion. Strength, courage, prominence, and character will only be built by becoming a well-respected anchor in the community which the business serves. The surest and fastest way to build a positive image as an entrepreneur is to get actively involved in the community. Join the local Chamber of Commerce, or perhaps serve on a board of directors or two. The management team must be encouraged to follow the leader. Soon, the business will be the main attraction when its services are needed.

Taking the road to transformation is the most rewarding of any possible route. This road is less congested, you set your own speed and you make your own rules. Being a transformer requires a high level of courage, grit, perseverance, faith and the attitude of a winner, even when you have just begun your journey. Pansies are for flower gardens, not business. As you drive your business on the road of transformation you earn the respect of your community, your colleagues and your loved ones. All along the journey you are rewarded with the trappings of success.

Our industry is one that has experienced major changes during the past few years. Some of these changes are for the better, while others have the potential to cause financial harm to the unwary business owner. For those who come out of the carpet cleaning industry you fully understand how forgiving that particular industry can be. The restoration industry, particularly the water damage field, is not as forgiving. It doesn't take too many slip ups to cause your business to come to a screeching halt.

Perhaps the biggest change and trend affecting our industry is in the way that services are purchased today. Not too long ago it was considered "Best Practice" to utilize an "outbound" sales strategy that included a mix of the following; market by way of mouth, television, postcards, email, personal visits, billboards, and so on. Today it is "Best Practice" to use "inbound" marketing strategies coupled with outbound. Inbound includes; social media, white papers, blogs, podcast, videos, e-news, SEO, e-books and so on. Inbound marketing has proven to be more cost effective with a greater ROI. Moreover, the uniqueness of inbound allows for engagement with the prospective buyers. Lest we forget the age old axiom—friends buy from friends!

Today's buyers are far different and much better equipped with high tech resources than buyers of five to 10 years ago. Today buyers are armed with computers, smart phones, social media resources like Facebook, Twitter and LinkedIn. Most buying decisions today have been made long before the buyer calls the restorer.

Today's consumers have more than likely already made the buying decision before having called you. I am reminded of a quote by the legendary master of the ice, Wayne Gretzky. Wayne was once asked; "Wayne how is it possible that you always seem to be at the right place at the right time?" His reply "I don't skate to where the puck is, I skate to where the puck will be".

An astute restoration owner will espouse this strategy and employ as much technological marketing and sales strategies as possible.

I strongly encourage that business owners get as much education as is possible before taking on the high risk game of water damage restoration. Having said that, I'd also encourage start-up restoration owners to carefully pick and choose their sources of education. The industry has a lot of useful information if you know where to look.

> *"It's vital to remember that it only takes one bad slip up*
> *to set back and possibly ruin a new startup company."*

We have all heard the old axiom—'fail to plan, plan to fail'. Some heed these words, while other scoff at their validity. Some are quite successful without having ever considered writing a plan, while others write elaborate plans worthy of the quill award, yet their business fails.

Never in my experience has this axiom been more true to life than in today's volatile cleaning and restoration industry. Can you build a successful business without a plan? Of course you can. Do your chances for long-term success as well as more profit for your business increase with a business plan? Of course they do. So at the end of the day, I'd say that anything you can do to improve your odds of long-term survival and success is worth the undertaking.

TWO TYPES OF NEW BUSINESS OWNERS

Through observation, I have discovered that there are two types of entrepreneurs. For discussion purposes, I have labeled them as "Type A" and "Type B" It is not for me to say which personality type works best. Well, on second thought, if pressured for an answer to which personality is best suited for starting a cleaning and restoration business I would unambiguously state that an amalgamation of both Type A and B would be advantageous to the business.

"Type A"

This entrepreneur possesses an infinite thirst for knowledge of the business he will be undertaking. He will study and learn everything he possibly can about the industry, local market conditions, the competitive field, necessary operating systems, etc. He will draft a business plan that could easily be mistaken for one generated by a Wharton School of Business Grad student, or a Team of MIT students working on the foundation of a multi-national fortune 500 company. All this preceding the day of hanging the open for business sign on their door. He may even dedicate some time working as a low paid intern in the employ of a restoration company to get a feel for what the industry is like.

The advantages that this individual has over "Type B" is that he has engaged in a very serious approach to the notion of opening a business. This of course is a favorable attribute, because starting a business truly is a more serious proposition than some may care to admit. This individual really does have a better chance of long-term success than "Type B".

However, on the downside, this individual may have the predisposition to over complicate or "over-think" the prospect of entering business. Worse yet, once established he may lose out on many opportunities that require lightning fast decision making. The highway to business ownership is littered along the way with businesses that were founded and lead by highly intelligent, big thinkers who for some reason or the other were never capable of turning the ignition, let alone taking the risk by adding a turbo charger to their vehicle called business ownership. This, in spite of countless hours of business planning, and weeks, perhaps months of dreaming of business success, is ultimately their undoing.

"Type B"

A little background on the "Type B" entrepreneur. This individual has a diminutive level of respect or use for serious business planning. He is an individual who lives by, and unfortunately, often time dies by, operating by the seat of his pants.

In the aviation world a pilot who flies with little regard or reference to available highly sophisticated avionics and navigational equipment is said to enjoy flying by the seat of his pants. For this aviator, life is simple. If the forces exerted on his body during flight give him the sense that the plane is banking sharply to the left, he simply inputs correction on the flying stick to the right. When he gets caught off guard and finds himself flying perilously through low level, soupy skies, he simply takes reactionary moves and dives, punching a hole through the clouds in hopes that he can get close enough to the ground without crashing, to find the nearest airport.

"Type B" is a reactive entrepreneur through and through. His personality allows him to sense trouble long before "Type A" does. However, due to his inability to take early corrective actions, he frequently finds himself serving as a full-time troubleshooter for the business.

This individual is one who bores easily, yet is typically gifted in the sense that he has a very creative mind and has qualities that make him an excellent visionary. One of the main factors that can have adverse negative effects on this individual is that his poor planning, record keeping, not so serious approach to his accounts receivables will at some time catch up to him. Another factor working against "Type B" is that he bores easily and often times will lose interest in marketing and sales programs and efforts before they have had a real chance of working.

I don't mind disclosing that I unmistakably fall into the "Type B" profile. It wasn't until several years into my business career that I took the time to write a formal business plan. Believe me when I say that "writing a business plan will do more for your business than anything else you do."

SITUATIONAL AWARENESS

This story was penned especially for those amongst us who occasionally find ourselves so narrowly focused on one area of life or business that we lose awareness of the situation in its totality.

In the world of aviation there are immutable laws of physics and aeronautical engineering that must be fully understood and embraced, lest we foolishly risk our lives.

The four fundamental forces that allow or disallow for flight;

• Thrust
• Drag
• Gravity
• Lift

Thrust is the force that propels the plane forward, while the opposing forces of drag are continually challenging the thrust. Much like a business, your vision is your thrust and many of the cumulative components of your business are your drag. Excessive employee turnover, poor customer service, under funding and many other operational factors are your drag, and have the latent power to negate your thrust which can lead to a stall.

In aviation, gravity is the law of nature that continually exerts a downward force that can only be overcome by generating adequate lift that exceeds the gravitational force. Much like an airplane, your business will also feel the effects of downward forces like gravity that oppose your lift, and forces of drag that resist your thrust. In our industry, vendor programs, lack of organizational skills, competing with some well entrenched brand leaders, are akin to this principal. It can be challenging at times to ascend for a sustained period of time.

In addition to understanding these four principals and how they relate to each other, a keen awareness of the plane's center of gravity is vital for safe flying, especially on climb out. Businesses also have a center of gravity, which most refer to as the core of the business. Much like flight, a business will also have forces that affect its ability to ascend to the top, or stall out and dive nose first into a grave yard spin, in the absence of balance. Oddly enough, air craft are all fitted with stall warning devices which audibly warn the pilot of an impending stall. Like the aircraft, a business also is equipped with warning devices. Like the balance sheet, poor morale, excessive customer service complaints, and so on.

I am reminded of the eloquent words of the late John Gillespie Mageeong in his poetic prose titled **High Flight**.

> *"Oh! I have slipped the surly bonds of Earth*
> *and danced the skies on laughter-silvered wings;*
> *Sunward I've climbed, and joined the tumbling mirth*
> *of sun-split clouds,—and done a hundred things.*
>
> *And while with silent, lifting mind I've trod the high, untrespassed*
> *sanctity of space, put out my hand, and touched the face of God."*

Thirty years ago, while working on some advanced flight training, I was fortunate to have retained a flight instructor who would teach me an important lesson that I still rely on today with my life and my business.

As a former Air Force fighter pilot, he had flown many combat missions over North Vietnam in the F4 Phantom. So as it went on this day, the cockpit housed two souls. A relatively new pilot on the left, abreast a man who had logged thousands of hours of flight time under some of the most strenuous conditions one could possibly imagine.

Shortly before we taxied out to runway 3-0 left, he had asked me what it was I was hoping to accomplish with his instruction. To which I answered, "I would like to build more confidence," as I had always feared something bad would happen during my routine flights. It might be encountering unexpected icing, an engine failure, a stall, or something as simple as running out of fuel, which, as hard as it may be to believe, does happen to many aviators. Until this day, there was this distant irksome fear that somehow prevented me from receiving the whole fulfillment that comes with flying.

We departed, flew around the local area for about an hour or so, while he silently observed my piloting skills.

Finally, I asked what he thought of my piloting. His reply was simple, yet 100 percent on target. He told me that there are two types of aviators. One is the type who flies only by the seat of his pants, and the other flies with situational awareness.

He went on to share his opinions of the two different, yet very distinctive types.

The aviator who flies by the seat of his pants, he said, was one who is reactive, while the pilot who possesses situational awareness skills during flight is one who is proactive and at the end of the day, under difficult flying conditions, is the aviator with the situational awareness skills that survives.

I said based on your observations of my piloting skills which category do you think I fall into? Without hesitation he told me that I was a by the seat of your pants aviator. He explained that there is nothing wrong with being a by the seat of your pants pilot. In fact, many aviators live for the feelings that come with pressure exerted on the body as well as the aircraft. Most aerobatic pilots live for this rush.

The biggest difference he noted was in the mortality rate of the two different types. He went further and cited several major aviation accidents that clearly were brought on by human error. The vast majority of those cited, were accidents where the pilot in command lost his or her situational awareness and the plane responded in kind.

Situational awareness as described by him was the "ability to become one with the aircraft"; to know her limitations, and more importantly, to know your own. In demonstration he took control of the flying machine and put her through some of the most unbelievable flight conditions imaginable.

I may have been somewhat anxious during his maneuvers, I did nonetheless remain confident in his abilities. I commented to him that I did not realize that this aircraft was remotely capable of executing these maneuvers. He replied that this plane is subject to three things. The laws of physics, confidence, and skill of the pilot in command.

The same applies with being an entrepreneur. You must possess the skills that are required to build a business and the confidence to execute the maneuvers that are proactive in nature.

A by the seat of your pants entrepreneur is one who waits for outside forces to cause him take corrective action. While one who possesses situational awareness, anticipates and takes corrective action long before any disasters can come to fruition.

Aside from the laws of business, it is the confidence and skills of the pilot in command of the business that determines the longevity of his career!

Safe flying

If you are really serious about taking your business to the next level and turning it into a **POWERHOUSE** cleaning and restoration business— visit showmemarketingsolutions.com Explore our one-on-one high level, innovative coaching program!

BEFORE STARTING YOUR BUSINESS

The more research and work you put into your business before ever starting the better. There are countless business failures in all industries, cleaning and restoration included, that can directly attribute their failure to lack of pre planning.

Where do I start?

If you are new to the cleaning and restoration industry, then right here with this book is a great place to start. It's not an all-inclusive guide; however, it will answer the vast majority of questions that a newcomer to this industry will ask. I feel that it is imperative that the newcomer take this information, couple it with basic research from other industries so that you can get a real feel as to how the service sector differs from the retail industry, for example.

I have witnessed all too many times where an entrepreneur will enter the cleaning and restoration industry with heavy experience in the fast food industry, as an example, and then endeavor to operate his cleaning firm as though it were a fast food outlet. It is true that both are businesses, and yes all businesses share similarities, however, the customers are different, employees are different, equipment needs are different and so on. Properly entering the cleaning and restoration industry requires an in-depth study of its history, inner workings, trends that may affect its operators, and so much more.

Long before ever making the firm commitment to enter business, one would be well advised to take some time to reflect on the tasks at hand. Operating a business, especially in the early years will require long hard workdays. Many inexperienced business start-up owners wrongfully have a blind faith that the money starts rolling in from day one. The truth is this; most new business owners find themselves laboring 16 to 18 hours per day for the first two to three years or longer just to get the enterprise up and running. And as far as the money, well for the vast majority of businesses it takes at least a couple of years before ever beginning to realize a profit. We had operated our first business for over five years before ever realizing that we were not generating a healthy profit. Sure, we had cash coming in, but more cash was going out.

Then there are the personal questions that one must ponder before making the commitment to move forward. Do I really have the stomach for business? This is one of the questions that isn't addressed in any business guide that I have ever read. Nevertheless it is one of the most important questions an entrepreneur must give some serious thought to. By stomach I mean this: operating a business requires that you play many roles and wear many different hats. You will be expected to lead, take risks, be creative, invest your hard earned financial resources, and win, lose, or draw, you will be the one held accountable. It takes a great deal of courage, perseverance, moxie, and dedication to be successful in business. **Yes, you can do it!**

An undesirable side effect of business ownership that is rarely discussed is the hardship caused on families. To step up to the challenge of business ownership in the absence of 100% commitment from your family is trouble just waiting to happen. Business ownership can and often times does lead to marital problems, even divorce. Imagine this archetypal scenario: Your spouse elects one day to start his own business. He gives you the cursory taster about the new-fangled business. Being the loving spouse that you are, you lend your approval and congratulate your better half for having the courage to step out on his own. So far so good—until sometime later you begin to notice that he isn't around a whole lot. At first you relish this respite. Soon he starts missing those special moments that the two of you had always shared together. He begins to miss the children's school events, their little league games, and all the other things that you now begin to realize a good spouse or parent couldn't possibly miss out on.

As if his absence isn't bad enough, he now starts dipping into the family nest egg to fund the new enterprise. How can one justify draining the family bank account, you might ask? For the entrepreneur it's easier than one might think. An entrepreneur with clarity can see the pot at the end of the rainbow through his vision of the business and knows in his heart that he can make this business thing work out—if only his spouse would cooperate with the financial backing. We all recognize that the outcome of mixing family and business in this way can be calamitous.

I was very fortunate that I had a wife who was also my business partner, on board 100% from the start. I would strongly advocate that the aspiring business owner spend the time early on in educating your family about what they can reasonably expect with the new addition to the family-named business.

So why then would one want to start cleaning and restoration business?

There are an assortment of people who might find themselves yearning to start a restoration business for one reason or another. Often these individuals can be grouped into a few generalized categories. Consider the following four groups of individuals likely to consider entering the realm of business ownership.

1) *Middle-aged executive caught in the downsizing vise.*

This individual perhaps had an enjoyable career in corporate America until budget cuts came along and he lost his job. Now he is confronted with unemployment. The options are few for someone his age and background and unemployment is on the rise. He turns to his best friend—Google—for help. There he surfs for diverse business opportunities and happens to stumble across the Cleaning and Restoration Industry as an option to fulfill his void.

The advantages for the unemployed executive are that he understands planning, budgeting, and possesses a management skills set that could get him started on the right track.

The displaced executive is coming from a big corporate business that was already established where his role was solely to manage the entire business or one of the businesses units. Now he is faced with running the entire business and will have to execute all of the decisions in the absence of the corporate support resources he once enjoyed. A new business will face abundant challenges as a start-up. Some of those are finding a market niche, developing a marketing and sales plan, human resource management, budgeting and at the same time striving to make a profit which may take years to do.

2) *The former customer of a cleaning and restoration company*

Here is a perfect specimen of someone who gets into the business for the wrong reason: This gentleman decides it's time to have the carpets in his home cleaned. He schedules the service and just so happens to be home on the appointed date and time of cleaning. The carpet cleaner is in his home working as hard as possible to clean with maximum results. All the while he is doing what he does best. **Delivering great, knock your socks off customer service.** After two to three of hours of hard work and painstaking attention to details the cleaner presents the owner with a bill for his services. After being handed a bill for $320 for three hours of work, the owner is livid. He cannot believe that he just paid some carpet cleaning businessman $320 for three hours of what looked to him to be easy work. This guy will then begin to ask 1,000 questions about the business. How long have you been doing it? How much did that carpet-cleaning thingamajig out in my driveway set you back? Soon after the carpet cleaning businessman has moved on, the homeowner now armed with a ten-minute question and answer session is ready to strike out on his own. Heck, he is only earning $18 per hour with his current employer.

As hard as this may be to believe, it's true and happens more often than you might believe. One of the reasons why this phenomenon materializes, is because we business owners have a tendency to make business ownership look easy. I once had a friend who was in the restoration business for three or four years. Here is his story which began with an insurance claim resulting from a water loss at his home which was easily worth $300,000. This gentleman had an illustrious career as a top manager for a larger corporation prior to being released from the corporation due to cutbacks. His severance package, according to him, was generous. A reputable franchise company had been called in to dry and repair his home through his insurance carrier. The owner of the restoration franchise happened to be on site many times during this drying project and was continuously asked questions by the inquisitive homeowner. Feeling like a high roller, the franchisee boasted about how much profit he was making in billing the insurance company. This in turn fueled this homeowner's curiosity.

Seeing how easy and lucrative the restoration business was, this gentleman went out and bought his own competing franchise at the cost of tens of thousands of dollars. This man spent the next three to four years struggling to make it work. I can attest to his struggles as I unwittingly became his mentor and educator. Time after time, I observed in disbelief as this otherwise very intelligent man made mistakes that even a neophyte would not make. Here he was, a franchisee of a well know franchiser, that incidentally has one of the best training programs available, floundering, and dead in the water. He bought into the allure of fast, easy and big money **Hook–Line–And–Sinker**. He has since sold his franchise. I often wonder if maybe I'll see him back in business after he has a new water softener installed, or calls the pest control guy.

3) Grew Up In the Industry

One who has grown up in the industry as a child of business owners is cursed with a double-edged sword. They are afforded voluminous advantages having grown up working, watching and learning the ins and the outs of the business first hand. This experience is invaluable, especially if they are the children of good business parents.

The disadvantages are plenteously problematic too. They grow up with conviction that the way the business is steered is the only way in which to conduct business. When the business torch is passed down to them, they continue to operate it just the way mom and dad had done so many times over the years.

Another impending difficulty when the next generation takes the helm and decides to overhaul the business with diminutive regard to employees, customers, insurance agents and adjusters, suppliers, etc.

I'll share an example: I had been marketing to and calling on this insurance adjuster located many miles outside of our primary market area for years with no results. I knew full well that his restoration company of choice was one of my competitors that was a family owned and operated business. I had rightfully presumed that in addition to his loyalty to this competitor, our distance from his base operating area was a detriment to my company. This competitor has a well-run company that for the most part provides a quality service. At any rate, the patriarch decided to take early retirement after having built this very successful cleaning and restoration business. Within a few months of his retirement, I got a call to do a job by the very adjuster that I had unsuccessfully market-ed too for the past several years.

Upon meeting at the job site, one of my first questions, more out of curiosity than anything else, was this; though I do appreciate the call and the opportunity to work with you, I must ask why now you have decided to give us a try. His answer was thought-provoking and certainly drives home the need for proper succession planning. He stated that he had always directed claims to the other company because the "old man" was easy to work with. He went on to expound that when the old man passed the business down to one of his many sons, things began to change. The son, now with his own agenda, became difficult to work with. Where the old relationship built on trust and understanding was one of give and take, the new relationship was one of mostly take with little give, on the part of the "Prodigal" Son.

4) Worked For Another Cleaning and Restoration Company

For those who are currently working for or have worked for another cleaning and restoration business and are in the process of opening their own business, I will offer these submissions:

Even with many years of experience working for other cleaning and restoration busi-nesses, there is much prep work to be done when it comes to starting your own business. If not handled correctly, your past employment experience can become a handicap.

I'm not wholly convinced that persons with this "I'm so much smarter than him" insolence are idyllic candidates for successful business ownership. My thought is this; if you worked for another cleaning and restoration business prior to striking out on your own and harbor ill feelings toward the former employer, you will be well served by making peace with yourself long before ever hanging out the open for business shingle. It will do you a world of good!

Starting a business with the brazenness of "I'll show him" or "I'll get even with him" attitude breeds unnecessary anguish, distrust and can consume your mind with thoughts of negativity, not to mention bringing bad karma to your new business. Entrepreneurs that fill their minds to capacity with positive thoughts, reverence for others, and associate with high achievers have a distinct competitive advantage and a clear point of differentiation that will reward them many times as their business develops and flourishes!

Believing in the Dream

I want to share a little secret with you. This secret involves a personal story and the use of a well-known phrase. But it is much, much more than that. It was shared with me by a stranger. I'll explain. Our precious daughter, Sara Fay, had been diagnosed with brain cancer when she was two years old.

She had a large tumor on her brain and thirteen smaller-sized ones on her spine. Sara underwent brain surgery, chemotherapy and full dose radiation in an effort to render the cancers harmless.

As loving parents this was the darkest period of our lives. We were blessed to have had some of the finest medical professionals in the country care for our daughter, and a very supportive family to help us through our crisis. Even so, the doctor's prognosis was that Sara would not likely live past five years of age.

Commonly used negative phrase –
"I'll believe it—when I see it."

One day we took our Sara and her sister to a local amusement facility named Miner Mikes. This house of fun is an expansive arcade center with games and rides as far as the eye can see, all for the enjoyment of children of all ages.

While we were moving about the facility from one game to another, an older gentleman unaccompanied by any children or grandchildren happened to approach us. Sara had lost all of her hair as a consequence of chemotherapy treatment, and at the time she had a feeding tube in her nose. It was apparent for everybody who would see her to know that she was a child who was suffering from cancer. This kind gentleman walked over to us and looked at our child. He began to speak to my wife and me about our daughter. He asked the emblematic questions that most people would ask. How old is the child, what form of cancer does she have, etc. This man was a very soft-spoken gentleman and his words were heartfelt and gentle. As he started to turn to walk away he glanced back at Sara and us and assured us that she was going to be just fine. His last words were; **You will see it—when you believe it!**

At the time his words were very calming, however they really never became copiously absorbed into my mind and heart until during our drive home that evening. It was during the drive that I realized that this stranger misstated the phrase. He had said, you will see it when you believe it. He surely must have meant you will believe it when you see it. After all, this is the only way that I had ever heard the phrase.

"You will see it when you believe it"

This idiom and its magical powers have given me more than I could have possibly hoped for in this lifetime. I unequivocally believe that understanding the power of this phrase, and when embraced and believed on a deep level, it will give life to even the weakest of people. This phrase, as you will note, is a simple reversal of the most commonly used negative phrase uttered by millions of people each day. Harness its awesome power coupled with hard work, dedication and a love for serving the needs of others, and you will achieve all the success and wealth that your heart desires.

"I'll see it when I believe it"

Understanding permits you to see the forest through the trees. Remember the feeling you got when Dorothy, Toto, the Tin Man, Scarecrow and the Cowardly Lion were in the Land of Oz? Each of these characters yearned for something that they believed could only be conquered by a visit to the Wizard.

Dorothy of course desired a ride home. The Tin Man needed a heart, the Scare Crow wanted a brain, and the Cowardly Lion sought courage. They traveled all the way to Oz, overcoming many perils and obstacles along the winding Yellow Brick Road. Within moments of the arrival into the fabled Oz, Toto tugs down the drape and there he was; the Wonderful, the all-knowing Wizard of Oz. He wasn't the great Wizard they had expected to see. No, on the contrary, he was merely a chap hiding behind a curtain. Yet, it was this artless man who bequeathed to each of the travelers what they so dreadfully desired.

The heart that he presented to the Tin Man wasn't a real heart. But yet, somehow, the Tin Man believed that he now had a heart. The same is true of the Lion and the Scare Crow. As for Dorothy, as the fable went she already possessed what she had wanted all along, to be home, and she arrived the moment that she believed.

In the 70's a popular musical group named "America" had a song titled the *Tin Man*. In it they sing "The Oz never gave anything to the Tin Man that he didn't, didn't already have." This phrase says it all!

Regarding the power of the phrase; don't just take my word for it, try this: Grab an index card and a pen. If you don't have one at this very moment stop reading and go get some index cards. Determine what you would like your gross revenues to be for your company in twelve months from the date that you are reading this. Make your number realistic, but don't be afraid to think big either. Remember – **Today Is YOUR Day!**

For the next 364 days remove this card from where you keep it stored. Look the card over and say out loud, "the gross revenues of my company are going to be $_____this year." Read this written statement first thing each morning when you arise from sleep and make it the last thing you say each evening before telling your loved ones good night.

When you travel, take this card with you. This system works like magic, it really does. **However, you must believe!** You can use this simple little gift for other wants in your life as well. Want a better relationship with your spouse? How about more quality friends? (Note: this system does not yield any results with know-it-all teen-aged children!) Give it a try—you have absolutely nothing to lose and everything to gain.

RUNNING THE BUSINESS – A THREE-HEADED MONSTER

Much of the content we have gone over so far deals with the restoration and carpet cleaning business specifically. However, a big part of what you will need to do as a business owner is applicable to every business in the world today. Running your business properly involves far more than simply knowing how to clean carpets and having the proper equipment for the job. You must understand day-to-day business operation as it relates to your employees, your bank accounts, and the laws of the area that you are operating within.

I termed this section a 'three-headed monster' because it has eaten up so many people over the years. In reality, the operational side of your business doesn't have to be intimidating at all. If you are well prepared before you get started and keep accurate records of everything that you do, you should be fine. Before we get too far along, I should identify the three heads of the monster.

- Human Resources
- Policy Manual
- Accounting

It is true that human resources and the policy manual go hand in hand and are part of the same department of operations. However, the policy manual is so important that it deserves its own designation to ensure that you pay proper attention to all that it means. If you are able to keep careful control over these three areas of your business on a daily basis, you will be amazed at how smooth your operation can be overall.

Basics of Management

Before we get into the particulars of the human resources and accounting operations of your business, some discussion of management is in order. As the owner of the business, you are the defacto manager until the business grows to the point that you can hire people to handle daily operations, although, as the owner, your position as lead manager will never really go away. Whether you have been a manager in various positions for many years or never managed an employee in your life, you will want to carefully read the following section to learn about how basic management practices translate to the cleaning and restoration business.

The Management Plan

Managing a cleaning and restoration business requires much more than just wanting to be your own boss. As a business owner you must display dedication and have persistence. Your management plan, along with your marketing and financial plan, will be the foundation of your business.

You must be capable of making decisions, some of which may have the potential to cause financial damage to your business.

Your building and equipment are resources of your business. So too are your employees. In fact, your employees are the most important resource your company has. It is crucial that you assess your management skills prior to hiring your first employee. Know what you are good at and what you are not so good at when it comes to managing employees.

This is a very important, yet often overlooked aspect of human resources that causes many cleaning and restoration business owners much grief. You will have to hire personnel that can supply the skills in the areas that you lack. Additionally, it is import-ant that you know how to manage and treat your employees. You must make them part of the team and keep them informed. Employees often times have excellent ideas that can lead to new profit centers for the business.

Your management plan should answer questions, such as the following:

How does your background or business experience help you in this business?

Do you come out of the service industry? If so, do you have a sincere appreciation for service workers and the work they perform? In my opinion, individuals who come out of the service sector have a unique advantage over those who don't, because they already possess the basic skills and understanding of the position and value of serving others.

What are your weaknesses and how can you compensate for them? As managers we all have weaknesses, and understanding this is the first step to becoming a virtuous manager. For me, at least in the beginning, my major weaknesses were numerous, in-cluding; thinking that all of my employees had to have the same work ethic that I had. If I was willing to work 16 hours per day I fully expected my employees to have the same mind set. What an erroneous demand that was! Employees of all businesses should be able to devote quality time with their families and friends and to pursue their hobbies, activities and personal interests outside of the work place, without the constant fear of losing a job because they have an outside life. Another chief fault that I possessed was the mentality that my employees were expected to do as I say, not as I do! In other words, my employees were to treat my customers with nothing less than 100% courtesy and provide exceptional work. This in and of itself is an exceptional management attri-bute by any measurement. However, at the same time it was acceptable for me to have the occasional outburst and speak negatively about a customer (never in the presence of a customer) but ostensibly acceptable in the presence of an employee.

Do you have prior management experience? If so, how have others rated your man-agement skills? Were you thought of as a jerk or did past employees consider you to be a fair-minded manager?

In my own case, had I been judged by a panel of employees many years ago, I'm em-barrassed to say, I would have been found guilty of management malfeasance for being a poor manager and perhaps some of the employees may have measured me as a jerk.

Some enjoyed working for me, many disliked working for me. I was moody, arrogant, sometimes seemingly unjustifiable, uncaring, and just no fun whatsoever to be around. I had one simple rule that I shared with all new employees on the first day they began their brief employment with me— **It's my way or the highway.**

Our 300% turnover rate was testament to my disinclination to budge. I had no problem finding good help. My problem was with keeping help. Thankfully, through much intensive training, a great deal of introspection, much study and reading on the subject of human management, I was successful in transitioning from a mediocre manager to one that had earned the respect of my employees. This transition is one of my most loved accomplishments of my career. My people mattered most.

Finding exceptional team members is a tough proposition. Most people don't grow up wanting to be a carpet or restoration technician. This is dirty, laborious work! However, there are great to excellent team members out there just waiting to be rescued by a business that **understands how to deliver great employee service!** For a complete Human Resource Manual designed for a cleaning and restoration business visit show-memarketingsolutions.com.

Who will be on the management team?

Your management team must be comprised of individuals that fully understand and embrace the vision that you have for your business. Your vision of course is your creation. It's the way in which you can see in your "mind's eye" exactly what the business will look like in one year, five years, ten years, etc. We'll discuss vision later.

Many business owners make the inveterate mistake of believing that they must hire people who they can control. Hire a department manager who will do his job, play by the rules, but above all else, keep him in the dark regarding the operations of the business. The business owner who operates with this attitude undoubtedly suffers from a smidgen of paranoia. Worse yet, his paranoia only generates animosity, then serves to fuel antipathy between his employees and himself.

There have been hundreds of books written on the subject of management. The general consensus with the majority of the books is that most employees want to do a great job, are willing to work hard, and will devote themselves to the company for which they work. Surprisingly, most employee's primary concern isn't monetary reward. The majority of employees, be it management or front line production workers, want respect and to feel as though they can contribute to the growth of the business.

Think for a moment of how popular organized sports are in America. People in the millions count themselves as die hard fans of NASCAR, football, baseball, hockey, and many other sports. We watch with intensity as our favorite teams play. We celebrate the victory and we mourn the defeats. We do all of this because somehow we feel connected to the team, even if we are thousands of miles from the action sitting in a comfortable recliner.

Business has many parallels with organized sports. A business must recruit and build a team that is comprised of individuals that are ideally suited for the positions for which they will be playing. The General Manager of the business may be likened to a quarterback of a football team. He or she must have a clear situational awareness of the game field. He understands the strengths and the weaknesses of his or her team. He is also aware of his opponent's or competitor's strengths and weaknesses. The quarterback's number one asset to the team is that he is capable of quickly calling plays. If one play doesn't work, he tries another.

Front line production employees can be compared to a NASCAR pit crew. The driver sits in the car and speeds around the track at break-neck speeds. He understands that at the very moment he needs to slide into pit alley, his crew must be ready to move in an instant. His pit crew fully understands the importance of getting the team car back on the track. NASCAR races are often times won or lost by a mere fraction of a second.

And finally, the person who makes it all happen—the owner. This guy is the one who quietly, from the sidelines, hires the best of the best to take his team to victory. The owner of a football franchise doesn't call down to the field telling the coaches which play to run. The NASCAR owner doesn't stand in the pit telling his driver which side of the track to run on. No, the smart owner hires people, then let's them do what needs to be done to win and he gives them all the glory. It is rare in sports or business that the highly successful owner takes the credit for the work of his team.

To build a winning team you must be willing to recruit persons with potential. You must be willing to step back and let your team do what it is they do best. You must have a game plan along with a play book. And finally, you must ensure that each of your players understand the plays!

Once you have assembled your team you must decide how you are going to compensate them for their efforts. What salaries, benefits, vacations, holidays, etc. Keep in mind that to recruit and retain a top-notch team you must be willing to pay well.

Every member of your team must fully understand exactly what is expected of them. The job description is a starting point, but ongoing training and developing their talents is also important.

What are your current personnel needs?

For a new startup business, the personnel needs will likely be small to conserve on finances. A carpet cleaning company starting out may have the following structure:

Carpet Cleaning Technician—1
Office Assistant—1

Many people in the cleaning and restoration industry may disagree with my reasoning for the new business owner to start his business with employees. Some will say that it makes more sense to start out as the owner operator then, as work flows in, begin to hire employees as needed. Where I disagree is that if a business owner has done all of the business planning correctly he should open from day one as a businessman and not an owner operator. The majority of owners who start out with this owner--operator mentality never quite seem to be able to get off of the truck.

Leadership

There have been hundreds of books written on the subject of leadership. There are countless seminars and clinics across the country that teach effective leadership. Even so, effective leadership is one of those illusive necessities of business ownership that many are just not proficient at fully grasping, even after years of trying. I consider myself to be a lifelong student of leadership development study and believe that it is imperative for all businessmen to always improve on their leadership skills. Your team deserves the best of you!

One of the key themes that I hope to drive home with this section is that the leadership of a cleaning and restoration company will directly affect all aspects of the company. There are many leadership styles, each with its own advantages as well as disadvantages. The point of this section isn't to suggest a leadership style for the reader. It is to simply exemplify the differences in style so that you, the reader, can have a better understanding of your own leadership style as seen from your employee's perspective.

A good leader will possess many attributes that his team will respect and admire, such as empathy, compassion, will, fairness, sureness, and resolve. A phrase that I have heard a time or two; I have worked for a leader or two that I would have taken a bullet for, and a couple who I could have given a bullet to.

The better you understand how your employees, customers, and the community around you view your style, the better armed you will be to shape a service company that is unique. It's this uniqueness or differentiation that can become one of many of your competitive advantages.

All great leaders are individuals who understand the importance that each of their own employees bring to their team. Leaders have no hesitation in seeking counsel of their employees on tough issues facing their organization. They take that information and couple it with their own thought process and make a decision. Once a decision has been made, it is carried out! Employees respect a leader who follows through on his decisions.

A perfect example of this admired style of leadership is the late Admiral "Bull" Halsey. During the Pacific sea battles of WWII, Admiral Halsey made it a habit to confer with each of his fleet commanders prior to taking action. Halsey would process this information. After that he would formulate a plan based on the information gathered from his team. Once his decision was made, it was final, no backing down or changing his mind even when at times the decision didn't look favorable. His men knew that the "Bull" had made his mind up and the plan would be carried out. After the war, many who served under him indicated that it was his confidence and resolve that they admired most, and that this trait is what allowed them to follow him, even at the risk of loss of life.

Leadership is so vital to the life of the business that it is worth the effort to always try to improve upon. You have some leaders who almost appear to be what some refer to as "Natural Leaders". I'm not convinced that there is such a thing as a natural born leader. I believe that the exceptional leader is one who makes it a habit to understand everything he can about his work force, then implements a style that brings out the best in those around him.

I have listed a handful of leadership styles. Perhaps you will see one that best describes yourself. If so, and if you believe that this style is not best suited for leading a fast paced service organization, then you really have a couple of choices. Number one is you could change your style. This is a very difficult thing to do and takes a considerable amount of time and discipline.

Another option is to hire people who possess the leadership skills that you believe will best help in taking your company in the direction that you would like. Even when hiring people to serve as leaders for your company, you still must demonstrate leadership to them as they will look to you for guidance and support. Personally, I believe that this is where most small business people fail. They understand that they lack leadership skills, yet are unwilling to bring people into the company who do know how to lead. If this describes you, wake up! There is nothing wrong or shameful about understanding that some people are better at some things than you are.

The Dictator - this leader is one who really thinks he knows everything. In fact it only takes a glance to spot this character. He is arrogant, unfriendly, talks too much and frankly, everyone around him resents his every move. His employees have been conditioned to stop using their minds and creativity as this would be a direct threat to the dictator. They are made to feel trifling and valueless. The financial compensation may be acceptable, and often times is the lone article keeping them with his company.

The Dictator manages his business like it is a small third world country, and his employees are the lowly peasants that make up the business. Often times these leaders will rule with terrorization and fear.

The Royal Elite - this is a leader who really thinks he is something special. His approach to management is as though their business is a particular class of royal dynasty where they are the self-imposed kings and queens, and their workforces are their subjects.

He also fancies himself as a puppet master who loves to toy with his subjects.

He lives in a delusional world, where to him it is perfectly acceptable for him to be seated on the royal jewels, all the while looking down upon his employees as they are paid so little that they can scarcely provide sustenance to their own families. He thumbs his nose towards any suggestions from his subjects as he cannot conceive the possibility that "one of them" could possibly know as much as him.

This is a leader who just does not get it. These are the jesters for whom the phrase the "blind leading the blind" was fashioned. While they may have a clear understanding of the technical side of the business, they lack any understanding of the business side of the business. This leader being "blind," is oblivious to his surroundings and simply instructs his people to follow suit as the business appears to vacillate meaninglessly.

The Rum Dumb - this is the leader who really isn't a leader in any sense of the word. Actually he would be doing well if he were ever able to achieve the status of dazed and confused. He only considers himself a leader by virtue of the fact that he owns the business. Pretty much everything he does is by happenstance. The whole world could be crumbling around him and all he can keep his mind on are the insignificant events that really have no impact on his business one way or another.

The Busy Body - this leader is characteristically one who possesses great skills so far as managing the diminutive details of a business. In fact he is likely one who pays very close attention to every detail of the business. The problem is that he has a very difficult time allowing the team to use its own God-given talents for the betterment of the business. Nothing is ever quite fast or good enough for this leader. They want to have their nose in everyone's business. Soon, employees begin to tire of having the busy body involved in every aspect of their position and move on to greener pastures.

Open Management versus Micro-Management

Every business owner is going to differ somewhat on the type of management system that they implement into their company. In the old days my style as previously noted was clearly one of a micro-managed type. For some this style works very well, but in my opinion takes a lot more work and effort than does one of an open style of management.

I'll expand a bit on my thoughts on the subject. I used to fill the management positions within our company under the assumption that one person would serve as the position holder's supervisor and ordered to keep open interaction between different positions to a minimum. My twisted thought back at that time was that by setting up our operational structure this way, we would reduce the possibility of managers sharing information between themselves that could possibly empower them and give them the tools they needed to leave our company and start their own competing company with information they gathered while working for me. My rule of the day was if an employee, be they management or production, asked a question, I'd immediately ask myself: "Does this person have the need to know?" This is a phrase that is drilled into all military men and women. And for good reason too, I might add. In the military many men and woman learn things such as ship movement, cargo on board, troop levels, etc. These things, though seemingly irrelevant to non-military personnel, can be dangerous in the hands of the enemy.

In retrospect the micro management system I utilized was futile. For one thing, I was taking way to much valuable time teaching basic aspects of our company to new hires that any one of our managers was perfectly qualified to do themselves. Another major shortcoming was in the mistrust that it instilled in all those who were part of the company.

Some years later I instituted more of an open management style process, which allows for a free flow of ideas, concepts, and brainstorming. This benefits the entire company and all those who are part of the team. Our management style today, I'm thankful to say, is not only radically different than just a few years ago, but the company has reached performance levels way beyond my own expectations. This has happened for several reasons: Each of our team members is carefully selected according to a high set of standards.

Once a team member has been recruited into the company, a carefully planned approach to training begins.

During the first day of orientation a considerable period of time is devoted to sharing my vision of the company with the new team member. As you will pick up throughout this book, it is my personal belief that your vision, if clearly seen in your mind's eye, then clearly and concisely put to paper and imparted to all team members will serve you well throughout the life of your business career.

I've known many cleaning and restoration operators who were super nice people, and they wanted only the best for their company. They even had dreams of how their business was going to improve their financial situation. Yet, when some of these same well-meaning individuals are asked to share their vision of their business, they give off a blank, deer in the headlights look. Think about it, how can your employees possibly know what you expect the business to look like if you don't share this valuable information with them?

Weekly Meetings

This is another subject that has been written about extensively. There are several ways that a company can conduct its meetings. I'll leave the formatting of meetings to the individual owners and experts on meeting planning, but will add this; if you don't hold regular staff meetings, you are missing the boat. We hold at least one meeting per week and try to keep them on Mondays, first thing in the morning. This has worked well because it gives us the opportunity to recap the previous week's work and to plan for the upcoming week. Plus as an added benefit, most of us are in a great mood on Monday!

During our meetings our office assistant takes minutes of the meeting. This, as you can imagine, is good because we start each meeting with the minutes from the last meeting. This method gets us off to a good start.

Meetings follow a planned agenda. Conducting meetings without a planned agenda will end up being little more than a 30-minute idle chitchat gathering, with the meeting taking no solid direction.

Something well worth trying is to switch the meeting planners from time to time. In our company for example, I typically serve as the planner. Because we are small business it doesn't take a lot of time or effort to perform the planning duties of meeting planner. Once in a while I'll switch things up and ask another member of the team to do the meeting planning. Not only is this fun for everyone else, it also serves to strengthen the morale of the entire team, not to mention the confidence it builds in the meeting facilitator.

Our meeting agenda is forwarded to everyone scheduled for the meeting through a simple word document that is emailed to everyone. In most cases we will have coffee and doughnuts or bagels available.

Meetings are the perfect opportunity to share and reinforce your vision with all attendees. We do this on the header of our meeting notification and also have the office assistant read the vision statement prior to the minutes from the previous meeting. This is an excellent way to brand your vision within your own company. When another team member has been selected to facilitate a meeting, I allow them to be 100% responsible from start to finish. Everything from the meeting agenda through the meeting assignments are their choice.

Human Resources

Notwithstanding all of your prodigious preparation and hard work, your overall success will be commensurate to the level of employees you hire to join your team. If you discover great personnel who are reliable and professional about what they do, your business has a great chance. If you simply hire the first people who walk through the door, you could be in trouble right away as poor employees will give your business a bad reputation in short order.

This human resources section is dedicated to making sure that you find exactly the right people for your cleaning and restoration business. There are four general portions of the hiring process that are covered in the following pages: recruitment, application, interview, and employment. None of these steps is all that difficult, but attention to detail will ensure that you don't have undue trouble along the way.

You will notice that there are a few scripts and sample interviews for you to put to use. While these should be a good starting point for you in your hiring process, you should of course tailor them to your specific business and add questions or tests that will fit your business specifically. Also, make sure to fine tune your interview and screening process as you go. Once you have a few interviews under your belt, revisit the questions that you are asking and get rid of those that you don't feel are serving any purpose. Before long you will be an experienced and confident interviewer.

Take your time to thoroughly read and understand this entire section. Finding good employees is the best thing you can do to get your business off on the right foot and headed down the path to success.

RECRUITMENT

The cleaning industry in general is not considered as a first choice for most employment seekers. Sadly, many candidates only knock on the door of a cleaning company as a last resort. In an attempt to counter this phenomenon we must attract only highly qualified clean-cut employees to start a trend that will become self-sustaining down the road.

People of high character usually associate with the same type of persons, so obviously it is an added benefit to include our employees in our recruitment efforts.

Position Advertising

Tools Needed:

Job opening position description steps:

The PM (Project Manager) will cooperate with the OPM (Operations Manager) to determine how many hours are available for the position available and any other special requirements that will be needed from the candidates applying for the position.

After job requirements have been determined, the PM will select the type of advertisement and recruitment tools best suited to attract individuals to the newly created or existing position. For further information on employment advertisements refer to the company forms manual.

Some of the many tools used for recruitment:

• Newspaper advertisement
• Employment fliers for grocery stores, laundromats, colleges, etc. Office marquee sign
• Employee referral
• Employment Fair Day

For many years our own service company would place small help wanted advertisements in the classified section of our local newspaper when we needed help. The response rate to our ads had never been all that good. It seemed like the caliber of applicant was usually less than desirable and often times these individuals lacked character. We even resorted to placing fliers using the same verbiage as the classified ads with little success.

One day we decided to experiment with the ads that we had been running. In the same newspaper on the same day we ran one of our regular help wanted ads. In addition we ran a newly designed advertisement that included graphics and a catchy headline. What we witnessed was quite astonishing. The new advertisement pulled 10 to one over the advertisement that we had run over the past few years. We also noticed a vast difference in the caliber of the applicants.

The cost to run the old advertisement was typically around $48 per run. The new advertisement, a two-column by five-inch display ad was around $110 to run.

An example of one of our old advertising pieces:

> *Carpet and restoration technician wanted for busy service company. Benefits including sick pay, retirement plan, and vacation provided. Candidates will have a clean background and must pass a drug screen. Call today or stop by our office. 634-3466. AERODRY 1221 Creek Trail Drive.*

Once we had the applicants in our office we noticed that the first questions they asked were about benefits, sick pay, and what type of vacation we offered. For the life of me, I just couldn't figure that one out. Why were they always interested in those things and never willing to see the potential in this job that we had available?

Then it finally hit me. They were only asking these questions because my own advertisement was encouraging them to do just that. My ad had no real reason for them to ask questions. It was no wonder I was only attracting the bottom of the barrel types. My advertisement was geared to get their attention, all the while not even getting a look from the quality of people I was searching for. Remember that advertising for employees isn't any different than advertising for customers. You must have a compelling headline, good copy, and a compelling reason to call.

Take a look at both advertisements below. You will notice that both ads indicate that we are looking for a cleaning and restoration technician. Both ads also indicate that we offer benefits of some sort. The big difference is that the display advertisement indicates that we are in search of individuals with star potential. Star potential = high achievers.

Underachievers, or people of low standards and little drive will likely not respond to the display ad because they know in their mind that they could not live up to those expectations.

> *Carpet and restoration technician wanted for busy service company. Benefits including sick pay, retirement plan, and vacation provided. Candidates will have a clean background and must pass a drug screen. Call today or stop by our office. 634-3466. AERODRY 1221 Creek Trail Drive.*

PM will submit the advertisement into the media chosen by following established procedures in section titled Staff Advertising in the Operations Manual. PM will also post a job opening notice with job description and income information onto company bulletin board in employee break room.

1. PM will authorize OA (Office Assistant) to distribute employment fliers to designated locations when a broadened recruitment effort is necessary. These fliers are placed on bulletin boards at no cost to our company and run for long periods of time. (They generally stay up until the store takes them down, or we remove them.) So obviously, we will frequently utilize this method for recruitment.

2. We are always accepting applications! Even when no actual positions are open within our company we still must keep up our qualified application file for when we do have an opening come available on short notice. Some individuals will call our office or drop in. In either case we will assume that we will have an opening

shortly if not presently. It never hurts to keep an active file of applicants who are qualified and ready to work.

THE APPLICATION

The application is the first tool that you have at your fingertips to use to find the right personnel needed for each specific job. Some of the areas to look at first when reviewing the application are: **reason for leaving present job, length of time at each establishment, how long did it take them to fill out application,** and **penmanship.**

It has been my experience that if a person puts down a reason for leaving such as "bad atmosphere", "they shorted me on my pay", or "poor management" that this person probably has a bad attitude and/or work ethic. By hiring someone who is a "bad seed" you may poison your entire company. When this happens, in some cases, you may have to fire an entire staff. Therefore, it is important to only hire people with the traits and skills you need along with someone who has high integrity, and of course you always want to hire someone who is honest and has a clean criminal background.

If someone only spends weeks to months with each of their employers, they are what I would call a "job hopper". Hiring this person can be risky. However, if you know that you only need someone for a short time, this may work out for you, so long as everything else checks out.

Another item to analyze is their penmanship and whether or not they filled it out at your location. An example of what I am speaking of is a guy that comes in and asks for an application. He takes it home to fill it out…or did he? One thing you should always require for applicants is a skills test. The skills test is filled out at the same time as the application, unless they take the application home to fill out, in this case, you would want to mention to them, that when they bring their application back, they will need to allow a little time to take a quick skills test. This test will not only tell you if they are qualified for the position, it will also tell you if they know how to read and write and what their penmanship is like. If they make a lot of errors, this is something that you should take into consideration. Another thing that should raise a red flag is when it takes an applicant an excessive amount of time to fill out a simple application. It has been my experience that this person will probably be the one that cannot accomplish simple tasks without a lot of supervision. This person may be lazy, or just not very quick on their feet. If you're in a service related business you know as well as anyone that time is money!

Procedure: Taking Applications

Purpose: To develop and maintain a selection of qualified candidates who want to work for our company.

Overview: Being a service company we are inevitably going to have some turnover. This being the case we need to always have a selection of qualified individuals who would be willing to work for our company. We know how important first impressions are, and want to take every opportunity we can to make a good first impression. We want to maintain a high level of friendliness and family-like atmosphere. Who knows, maybe that person will be so impressed with our attitude that they will tell a friend about us.

Tools Needed:

a. Application form
b. "Thank you for your interest" letter
c. "Before you fill out this application" letter

Steps: Company uses a standardized employment application. This form must have one of our "Thank you for your interest" and our "Before you fill out this application" letters attached to it. The Thank you for your interest letter is used as a brief introduction of our company. The before you fill out this application letter serves as a guide to the required prerequisites of employment with our company. Both pieces should be stapled to the application on the front cover of the application in the upper-most left hand corner. (Letter should be stapled on the front of the application for reading before filling out. Make sure that the applicant takes both form letters with them upon exit.)

When an applicant first walks into our office, the OA, or whoever happens to be up front will use the following format:

Office: Good morning/afternoon, how can I help you?

Applicant: Yes, I'd like to apply for your position.

Office: Great, will you be filling it out here?

Applicant: Yes

Office: I'm (Office Rep's Name), what's your name?

Applicant: response

Office: Okay (applicant) if you would follow me please, I'll take you on back to our employee break room where you can fill out your application.

After the applicant has been seated. Can I get you a soda or a cup of coffee (applicant)? Note: Always make sure we have soda available before asking the question.

Office: (Applicant), I'm going to go back up front for a few moments. If you finish before I get back, please feel free to come up front with your completed application. Otherwise I will be back to check on you shortly.

Office: Do you have any questions before I leave?

Applicant: If no, then resume your normal activity. If yes, then address applicants question or concerns.

About every 10 minutes go back and check on applicant. At this time, you may inquire as to how they are doing.

When applicant has finished filling out the application, if we want to fill an immediate position, ask them if they would like to schedule an interview for the position. Choose a date and time when we can conduct the interview and go ahead and tell the applicant at that time when the date and time of the interview is.

NOTE: NEVER SCHEDULE A WALK- IN INTERVIEW!

For the applicant write the information on the back of your business card as follows:

Interview Time: 9:00 a.m.
Interview Date: April 4th

Write the interview date and time on the top blank space on front side of application. Use pencil only on the completed application. We would not schedule an interview if applicant leaves with the application. Interviews can only be scheduled after receipt of completed application.

We obviously would not want to schedule an interview with someone who was not qualified, so refrain from scheduling an interview with unqualified candidates.

Applicant: When will I be hearing from you?

Office: We will contact you if we need to interview you or if we need any additional information. Thank you for applying with us!

The staff member that has the contact with the applicant must, with sticky notes, explain why they felt the person was not qualified for employment. i.e. extremely over-weight, or perhaps the applicant told you they do not have a reliable vehicle that they could use each day, or the applicant is at an age that in all likelihood would not be capable of the strenuous routine of the position.

Company prohibits the use of any written or verbal derogatory personal remarks!

Never make any notations regarding race, personal appearance, or anything else that could be taken as personal. A good rule of thumb is simply that if it sounds wrong, then it probably is.

Unqualified applicants that we will not be interviewing will have their applications discarded and shredded.

Applicants that show potential will be filed in "Application File." This file is stored in the current employee file drawer until we are ready for an interview.

Applicants that appear to be qualified and show potential will be sent a "Thank you for Applying" letter the day following their visit to our office. This letter is sent only to those qualified applicants that have not been scheduled for an interview.

Qualified applicants will be shredded once we have called the applicant for an interview and they decline our offer. Because an applicant declines our offer of an interview does not necessarily mean that we will not hear from them at a later date. Often times an applicant has already taken a position elsewhere before we have an opening. But, because we want only active files, we still would destroy the application. They can, however, reapply at a later date.

If a caller states that they were contacted by our office in the past and offered an interview, but they declined it, and now would like to take advantage of an interview and we are indeed hiring, go ahead and schedule the interview because this person was obviously a qualified applicant or we would not have called them for an interview in the past.

If a caller states that they saw our ad for help wanted and that they have already applied, tell them that we, in all likelihood, still have their application on file and will call them if we need to schedule an interview. (For unqualified applicants only)

On occasion, an applicant will arrive at the office with a prepared resume. This is certainly a nice thing to have, however we still must have a completed company application on file.

>Applicant: I brought in a resume and would like to inquire about employment.

>*Office: Great, your resume will certainly be helpful in our decision-making process, however, we still would like for you to complete one of our company employment applications. Will you be filling it out here?*

Procedure: Initial Telephone Qualification Interview

Purpose: To qualify potential employees over the phone as opposed to allowing them to visit the office and use up valuable and costly employee time, especially if they are obviously unqualified. Also, this procedure allows us the opportunity to demonstrate our professionalism to potential employees.

Steps:

1. When talking to potential applicants over the phone simply follow the outline of this script.

>*Office: Thank you for calling AERODRY, this is _____, how may I help you?*

>Caller: In most cases the caller will state having seen an advertisement or flier about the job opportunity, and will ask to be told about the position.

>*Office: I can help you with that; may I ask you a couple of questions first?*

Note: In most cases, the caller will say sure

>*Office: Do you have a reliable vehicle?*

Note: If the caller says he/she doesn't have a reliable vehicle reply as follows:

>*Office: Our company policies require that our employees have a reliable vehicle. Though you may not drive your car every day, you must be capable of being placed in line for driving duty rotation with your co-worker if we ever needed you to drive.*

>*Office: Do you have a working telephone?*

Note: If response is no or if they are expecting to get a phone soon, respond as follows:

Office: Although most employees are assigned pagers for business use it is pol-icy for each of our employees to be accessible by the company in the event of emergency work or when scheduling changes occur. We expect our workers to have a phone number where we can reach them. Because much of our work is on short notice, we do not want answering machines, or to relay messages through a third person like relatives or friends.

Sometimes a caller will ask why we have such a policy or policies. The stock re-sponse should be; again, there are just basic requirements that our company feels nec-essary for the right type of candidate for our positions.

If the caller has met, or indicated willingness to meet, the requirements of vehicle and telephone then move on to the following:

Office: How many hours per week are you looking for in a job?

Caller: If they need more hours than what we have available for the posi-tion then respond as follows:

Office: This is a part time job. Our employees normally work between 20 and 34 hours per week. Any time over that cannot be guaranteed. (Of course if the position is a full time position then by all means let them know. All information about the job opening will be available from the GM/OPM and will be posted on the break room bulletin boards.)

At this time, if the caller shows an interest, give them the starting through the maxi-mum pay scale range for the position. Briefly give an explanation of the job description, type of availability required, travel requirements, training programs, etc.

Note: Often, callers will attempt to interview the company over the phone and may try to extract more information during the telephone conversation than is normally necessary for making a decision to come to the office for an application. While un-derstanding that answering a couple of routine questions is proper, beyond this, po-tentially places the company in a position of divulging privileged information and is a non-productive use of employee time. Our company will answer two (2) questions and no more. We will answer questions which do not place the company in a compro-mising position.

Commonly asked questions to avoid answering include:

1. Location and names of customers
2. Pricing or methods used to price services
3. Number of employees
4. Number of accounts
5. Team compositions
6. Supplies used

COMMONLY ASKED QUESTIONS/ANSWERS FROM PHONE APPLICANTS

Caller: **Do you offer benefits?**

Office: Before answering this question, be sure to know the answer. Many of our positions from general laborer to part time or stand-by restoration employees may have no benefits. Yes, we do offer a benefits package. We have sick pay, paid vacation program, and an attractive pay incentive program, as well as a discount on our services and products.

Caller: **How often are you paid?**

Office: Paydays are on the 15th and the 30th of each month.

Caller: **Will I work evenings or weekends?**

Office: Answer this question using a job description or the job bulletin.

Caller: **Do you hire husband/wife teams?**

Office: While we would consider such teams, if equally qualified, we would not guarantee that both would be working together on every job.

Applicant Reference Results

During my 20 plus years as a business owner I've made many hiring mistakes. I've also been fortunate to make some good hiring decisions as well. Looking back, I realized that the vast majority of my hiring mistakes were the result of one major weakness on my part. I hired on emotion! Emotion is a very powerful trigger during the hiring process for the unwitting manager/owner. It is very easy for the owner/manager to get swept off of his feet by a well-oiled, highly polished applicant. Lord only knows how many individuals (especially females) I've personally hired over the years, simply because they complimented me on my attire, looks, or success.

To be clear here: by emotion I'm speaking of the feelings that you receive from an applicant. I consider this a bit different than "Gut Instinct." Gut instinct, on the other hand, is a gift that all human beings possess that can be one of your greatest friends if you are open to listening to it. I have found that it is rarely wrong. Your gut instinct is that little inner voice that whispers in your mind..." hey something just isn't right with this." Or perhaps, "I've got a great feeling about this."

No matter how intelligent and friendly an applicant may appear to be in person, you must always do your due diligence prior to making a commitment to hiring any individual. While there is no guaranteed way of ever knowing for sure about the history of any individual, conducting a reference investigation will lessen the risk of making a bad hiring decision.

Once you get a completed application and you have reviewed all of the applications, and the interview process is complete, it is time to check the potential candidate's references. You will find the information that you need either on the applicant's application or on their resume. During the interview process is the appropriate time to ask for references if they were not already furnished. When calling former employers, some of the most important questions are:

- Was he/she reliable (Did he/she miss a lot of work due to illness and/or personal problems?)
- How did he/she get along with co-workers?
- Is he/she eligible for re-hire?
- Did this employee file a workers' comp claim?
- Was this person able to work independently or did they need constant supervision?
- Was this person good with your customers (if applicable)?
- Would you consider this person trustworthy?
- On a scale of 1-10 (10 being the highest) how would you rate this person overall?
- What was this person paid when he/she worked for you?

RELEASE AND AUTHORIZATION FOR BACKGROUND AND REFERENCE INVESTIGATION

Getting a background check in addition to checking the potential applicant's personal references and former employers is also a very important step in the employment process.

The right time to have the potential employee sign this form is after an interview (only if you think you may consider this person for the position). By signing this authorization, you are granted permission by the applicant to run any/all necessary background checks including but not limited to: criminal history, credit history, driving records, salary information. It will depend on the position the applicant is applying for how thorough of an investigation you will need to do. For example, if this person will be driving your vehicle(s) on a regular basis, you will definitely need to get driving records.

If, after reviewing the driving record, you see that this person had a DWI two years ago, you will probably not be able to hire him, because of insurance reasons. This is something you would need to check on with the insurance company that carries your automobile liability insurance. My insurance company will not insure someone with a DWI within the last 5 years! (I was surprised to hear this, but this is information that we, as employers, have to know in advance).

What would happen if you hired this person without doing any checks, especially a driving record, and the very first day on the job he gets into an accident where, because of a reckless act on his part, kills a passenger in another vehicle? The answer is: You will probably be out of business within the next few months because you are going to be sued!! And, to top that off, your insurance company may not cover the loss. If they do, they will promptly cancel your insurance. Good luck, finding another carrier!

Again, I would like to stress the importance of being thorough on your background and reference checks BEFORE you decide to hire someone. You will save yourself so much time, effort, and headaches in the long run by following due diligence in this regard.

Checking Applicant References

Purpose: To provide a guide for checking potential employees prior to their being interviewed. This allows the company a chance to prepare for the interview and to confirm the potential of an applicant.

The second method is done by sending an applicant-signed release of information form directly to the former employer in hopes that they will take the time to complete and return to our office.

This method, though effective, requires the cooperation of the applicant and the former employer. It is more costly and of course time consuming. And, as with the telephone reference check, most employers will be reluctant to discuss problem employees.

Overview: In today's litigious society most employers will not be willing to provide any more than confirmation of work history. If there is no direct supervisor listed on the application, then a request should be made for the human resources department (applicable to large companies). The OPM will be responsible for conducting the applicant reference check.

There are two basic methods for checking employment references. The most popular way, and certainly the quickest and least expensive of the two, is by direct contact via the telephone with former employers. With this method we simply make phone contact with the former employer and ask a few questions and in minutes the reference check is completed. The drawback to this method is that often times, former employers are not willing to discuss former employees, especially if they were problem employees. Many companies will simply tell you that they are only willing to verify employment and will release no further information.

Note: Some applicants will ask that you not contact certain past employers. Our application has an area on it that the applicant can check if they do not want us making contact with certain former employers. Please be cautious not to contact those requested by applicants. Doing so could cause serious legal problems! Also keep in mind that the applicant may be trying to hide something with this request.

Tools Needed:

a. Completed application with applicant signature on the release of information line.
b. Blank legal pad
c. Standard employee reference check form

Steps:

1. The first step in the process of reference checking is to have the reference check forms filled out in advance so that we are prepared when we speak with the former employers.
2. If the reference checks will be conducted via telephone we will use the reference form format. Simply ask the questions as they are laid out on the form, and note the

former employers' answers verbatim in the spaces provided. The applicant's signature on the employment application will serve as a release of information.

3. If an employer is reluctant to give information via the telephone then we will have to proceed with faxing or mailing an applicant signed reference check form. When mailing a reference form to former employers, include a pre-stamped company envelope with our return address.

4. Prior to conducting an applicant interview, try to contact as many of the references prior to the scheduled interview as possible. A minimum of two successful reference checks is required prior to moving forward with the pre-hire process.

5. Contact the supervisor on the application; however, if there is none listed, ask for the human resources department or the manager.

Reference Check Script

Office: Good morning/afternoon, may I speak with the manager or the person in charge of human resources for employment verification purposes? (Once speaking with the person) Good morning/afternoon, I'm (name/title) with (your company name) in (your town's name), I am calling to verify employment of (applicant name). (Applicant name) has applied for a position with our company and I would like to ask you a few questions regarding his/her employment with your company.

Former Employer: If yes, then proceed with questions in the order they are laid out on the reference form. At the conclusion of the telephone conversation thank the employer for their assistance in providing the information requested.

If no, then ask if they can, at the very least, verify the applicant's employment dates, pay rate, and if he/she is eligible for re-hire.

Whichever is the outcome of your call to the former employer, keep in mind that many business's and especially larger institutions have a no-tell policy.

I have usually had pretty good luck even after being told that "we cannot give out any information." I will usually respond to this statement by stating that as a business owner, I certainly understand your position. However, my questions and your answers are in the strictest of confidence and would not be shared with the applicant or anyone else for that matter.

Procedure: Scheduling the interview via telephone

Purpose: To efficiently screen applicants for potential hire and employ with company. This is done to prevent under-productivity from occurring due to unscheduled interviews happening. Also allows the company adequate time to check the applicant's background prior to an interview.

Overview: When at all possible, interviews should be done on the same day and time. Obviously, due to manpower restraints, it may be necessary to do it on special occasions. Typically, interviews should be conducted on Wednesday afternoons, 1 p.m. to 5 pm. This allows for assessing the application prior to the Friday a.m. orientation start. A normal interview will last from 30 minutes up to an hour, not including a one-hour period prior to the actual interview, which is time allowed for interviewee to take pre-hire test. OPM is responsible for conducting interview.

> *Office: (Applicants name) this is (name of company rep and position) with AERODRY in Jefferson City. You applied for employment with our company on (date) for the position of (position desired). Are you still seeking employment?*

> Caller: If answer is no, ask him/her if they wouldn't mind sharing their reason for no longer being interested? Make note on a separate sheet of paper so we can attach to the application for review.

> *Office: Would it be all right with you if we keep your application on file for a while and check back at a later date if we find another opening? If applicant still shows no interest, thank him/her and destroy the application. If they state that it would be all right then make a note on paper that the applicant is not interested at this time with their reason, and file into application file located in Human Resources drawer.*

> *Office: If yes, reply, "Great!" Then as follows: (Name), the reason for this call is because our company is interested in discussing available job opportunities with you. Our next available interview date and time is (always try to schedule on Wednesday between 1 p.m. and 5 p.m. at thirty minute increments). We would like you to come in at (pm). Will that work for you?*

Note: If applicant states this is not a good time, advise that we have interviews on Wednesdays and we could do the interview the following week. No exceptions without the consent of our OPM for day to conduct interviews.

Note and confirm the interview with applicant and mark the date and time of interview on the top of the application.

Office: (Applicant's name), although your interview is schedules for (__ : __) pm on the (date) we would like you to arrive one hour prior to that time to complete a couple of questionnaires AERODRY administers prior to interviewing. That being the case we would like to see you at (time) on the (date).

Office: If applicant has no questions about the date or time to arrive at office, close by stating following: (Name), Thank you and we are looking forward to seeing you then. Bye.

Place the interview information and application into the OPM basket. Schedule interview in computer using your calendar.

Pre-hire Testing ARD (Applicant Risk Detector) & RT (Reliability Test)

Purpose: To assist in the direction to choose the best candidate for available positions, (your company name), will require each applicant that shows potential for employment to take the ARD/RT test. These tests will provide information concerning the dependability, integrity, and aggression level of each applicant. These tests also allow our interviewer the opportunity to address any of the questions and the applicants' answers to the questions during the interview. These tests are only administered to applicants that have been scheduled for an in office interview, and are given one hour prior to the interview.

Tools Needed:

a. ARD/RT test
b. Ballpoint pen

Steps:

1. Test is to be prior to the interview, in a quiet room with no distractions.
2. Provide applicant with a ballpoint pen to ensure clear markings on the answer sheets.
3. Distribute the test and have applicant complete the information on the front page of the test. (i.e., name, social security number and date.)
4. Introduce the tests to the applicant. (Applicant's name), this questionnaire is de-

signed to assess your opinion of different types of work-related behaviors and atti-
tudes. There are no right or wrong answers. Responses will vary depending on each
individual's personal beliefs. Remember, there are no right or wrong answers, so
please be as honest as possible. Your unique style of thinking about or handling various types of work related situations might be exactly what the job requires. Remember, your first response is often your most candid and honest response.

5. After the applicant has read the directions, ask, "Are there any questions?" If there are
no questions, state, "There is no time limit, so please take your time and make sure
you answer every question. Remember to think about the questions as they relate to
your day-to-day working situations and not situations outside of the working environment. You may begin."

6. Once the applicant completes the test, ask him/her to make sure he/she has answered every question. When the test is turned in say, "Thank you. We appreciate
your taking the time to complete this test."

Prior to the interview the interviewer will have scored the test and determined any
questions that he needs to address with the applicant during the interview based on the
answers given on the tests. An example might be if the applicant answered that it was
normal to use illicit drugs. The interviewer might ask the applicant to clarify what they
meant by that answer.

7. Before testing, you should be familiar with the test and grading instructions. Be prepared to answer any questions that may be raised.

8. After test has been graded, the OPM will grade the test using the procedures outlined
in the administrator's manual.

9. After the interview has been completed the test will be filed into the Human Resources File under Pre-Hire Testing.

A Word of Caution! Some states may prohibit the use of Risk Assessment Testing.
Seek legal advice before implementing this type of testing into your business.

CLERICAL SKILLS TEST

When in the need of clerical staff, our company utilizes a computer software skills
test to determine what the individual understands relating to the products that we use
on a regular basis: PowerPoint, Word, and Excel. From experience we have found that
just by asking or even looking at someone's resume' does not automatically mean that

this individual will know how to use these applications. In some cases an individual will put down that they have experience with these items, only to find out later, that they have not used ANY software applications within the last ten years. In a case like this, you would literally have to retrain this person, because after so much time they might have forgotten most of the things that they learned due to lack of use and the fact that there are constantly new updates to software programs.

As a top-notch company that wants to be better than the competition, you would want your office/clerical help to be the most knowledgeable in the different types of software that your company uses. This person should be the one that other employees can come to as well to find the answers to their questions relating to the software.

In-office Interview & Guide

Purpose: To assist our interviewer in gaining as much pertinent information regarding the candidates' work and personal traits as is possible. By interacting in a one-on-one relationship during the interview, we are better prepared to make an informed hiring decision. To ensure a successful interview the following points should be observed.

A. Show a genuine concern and interest in the applicant and what he has to share with us.
B. Stay in control of the conversation and display confidence when asking questions.
C. Make direct eye contact when asking questions.
D. Stay on track, do not become too personal with candidate
E. Cease the interview if at any time the candidate shows lack of interest.

Note: To stop an interview; inform the applicant that you feel like you have all the information that you need at this time and that we will be back in touch should we desire any further information. The interviewer should follow the guide as it is laid out.

BE SURE TO TAKE NOTES!!!

This guide has been arranged in the following sequence:

A. Greeting the candidate
B. Putting the candidate at ease with brief small talk
C. Giving an overview of what we expect to accomplish from the interview
D. Eliciting information about the candidate

E. Describing the job

F. Answering questions

G. Closing the interview

H. Grading the candidate

Greeting the candidate:

OA will walk out to reception area of office to greet the candidate. OA will introduce herself to the candidate with a handshake (good morning/afternoon) (applicants first name) I'm, (first and last name)...and (position with the company) I will be getting you prepared for you interview today with (interviewers name and position). If you would follow me please we will go to a quiet area where we won't be disturbed.

Once you have the candidate seated, ask if he/she would like something to drink. If so, ask the OA to fix it for them, and be seated across the table from them. (Always be sure we have a soft drink or coffee before offering.)

Putting the candidate at ease with small talk:

The first four or five minutes should be spent relaxing the candidate with talk about weather, sports, or other subjects that are general and light.

Giving an overview of what you expect to accomplish during the interview:

(Candidates first name) as you know, we are interviewing candidates for the position of (position as taken from job description). What I would like to gain from this interview is a general sense of your experience, your background and strengths that you feel you could bring to our team.

If a candidate persists in asking too many questions at this point, politely tell them that you will be happy to answer any questions they might have at the end of the interview, but in the meantime you have some important information to gather first.

Eliciting information about the candidate:

As you are asking the questions, be sure to use the candidate's first name often.

1. What kind of people do you like to work with?

2. At your last job, what was your title and what were your functions?

3. What did you like most about this job?

4. What did you like least about this job?

5. Why did you leave or why do you want to leave your existing job?
6. Did you like your supervisor? If not, why?
7. What are you looking for in your next job?
8. What are you looking for in your next supervisor?
9. What do you like about this job position?
10. Who or what has been the greatest influence upon your career?
11. Do you have a salary goal?
12. Do you have a personal job goal?
13. What motivates you?
14. What are you confident doing?
15. How would you describe yourself as a person?
16. If you had your life to do over again, what would you do differently?
17. What gives you the greatest satisfaction on the job?
18. What frustrates you the most?
19. How do you cope with your frustrations?
20. Please describe your view of what defines a "good employer"
21. Do you believe in getting even? Why not?
22. What do you enjoy doing in your off hours?

23. Why do you think we should hire you?
24. Do you consider yourself a pessimist or an optimist? Share an example please.
25. Are you driven? For example, when you want something, do you put a plan of action into place to get it?

   If yes, to question 25 follow up question

26. Since you are applying for a position with our company, what type of plan did you put into place to improve your chances of getting hired?
27. What type of research have you conducted on our company or the job that you are applying for?
28. Do you have any questions about our company?
29. Do you have any questions about me as your prospective boss?
30. Do you have any questions about our company?

Describing the job:

   Give a brief overview of the following topics; using job description, policy manual and any other material as needed to show the candidate that we do indeed have a structured program.

1. Our history
2. Services offered by our company
3. Pay structure of position
4. Advancement opportunities (review organizational chart and job description to give an overall view of how our company fits together and possible promotional paths for him/her.
5. Pay dates
6. Holiday and vacations
7. Attendance requirements
8. Uniform policy and personal appearance
9. Medical benefits
10. Profit sharing programs

At this point again ask our candidate if he/she has any questions. Be truthful when answering questions and do not attempt to sugar coat the position. We obviously do not want to scare off potential candidates with the thought that the work will be unbearable, but at the same time remember, once they become an employee they will discover everything about the job and our company so please be completely honest about all aspects of our company. This is a good place to work, if this candidate does not accept employment with us at this time for whatever reason this is OK. It is much better to know that they were not interested from the start rather than after having them employed for several weeks just to quit because they realize that this job is not what they envisioned.

Before closing the interview read the candidate our Zero Tolerance Drug and Alcohol Policy

Our company has contracted with an independent laboratory-testing center for random drug testing of all employees, up to and including all members of management, including the president. If you test positive for illegal drug use, you will be terminated immediately. If you use drugs you will not work for our company.

Policy on DUIs. A DUI or OUI conviction during your employment will result in your immediate termination.

Any employee charged with illegal possession, use of, or sale of drugs by any city, state or federal authority would result in immediate unpaid suspension from active employment, pending conviction or exoneration.

Any employee suffering from job performance difficulties, which may be related to chemical dependency problems, may voluntarily discuss these problems with GM.

The consumption of alcoholic beverages during lunch hours is prohibited. The consumption of alcoholic beverages prior to reporting to work is prohibited for both day and night employees.

Closing the interview:

Give the candidate a time line of approximately when we anticipate needing to fill the position and when we plan to have a decision made as to who will be chosen for the position.

After candidate is done presenting questions, indicate that at this time the interview is concluded. Stand up and shake hands with the candidate and thank him/her for their time and for coming in, and escort them to the front door.

SAY ABSOLUTELY NOTHING ELSE!!

GRADING THE CANDIDATE:

Does the candidate appear interested in our company and the position?	Yes / No
Did the candidate answer questions with straight forwardness?	Yes / No
Did the candidate appear to be contradictory in answering questions?	Yes / No
Did the candidate avoid direct eye contact?	Yes / No
Did the candidate appear to try to hide something from the interviewer?	Yes / No
Did the candidate appear overly nervous?	Yes / No
Did the candidate appear to lack depth?	Yes / No

The following topics are graded "G" for good and "P" for poor.

Personal Appearance

a. Hair   G / P
b. Clothing   G/ P
c. Hygiene   G / P
d. Posture   G / P

Attitude

a.	Speech	G / P
b.	Interest Shown	G / P
c.	Response to Questions	G / P
d.	Punctuality	G / P

Interviewer's comments:

Based on my interview:

- I do recommend this candidate for a position with company.
- I do not recommend this candidate for a position with company.
- I feel that another interview is required.

Interviewer _____   Date ___/___/

Making the Offer of Employment

Purpose: To have a system in place to notify successful candidates that we have decided to hire them into our company.

Overview: The checking of criminal records, driving records, past employer's references, physical and drug screen, and all the other necessary pre-hire work is finally completed. Now is the time for the potential employees we have been waiting for. It is the time to make an offer of employment. Up to this point much hard work involving several staff members has run smoothly to ensure a rapid turnaround time from application to hiring. Undoubtedly, the new employee has been impressed by our professional service and our seamless systems. It would be a real shame at this time to blow it by not feeling a real sense of accomplishment that the company is bringing a new team player to the organization. This is a real sign of growth and success on the part of our entire operation. Please don't be afraid to let the new employee in on the good news when we make our offer.

Tools Needed:

a. Employee application

b. New employee service file with all paper work that has already been completed.

c. All forms and documentation that will be filled out during the hiring meeting.

d. Tracking applicant to employee status form.

Steps:

1. OPM will make contact with applicant via telephone to schedule the offer of employ-ment meeting and will handle the entire process of making an offer of employment. This applies to production employees. For office employees the Office Manager will make the offer. Make sure to note time and date of meeting with a sticky note and place on the outside of applicants service file. The following script will be used for telephone contact and offer of employment:

   Office: Good Morning/afternoon (applicants name), this is (company reps name and title). You have applied with (Your Company) for the position of (job title). Are you still interested in joining our team?

   Applicant: If yes, then proceed.

   Applicant: If no, inquire as to why no longer interested and write down the reason(s).

   Office: Great, we are very excited about having you join our team and would like to have you visit our office on (date and time. Note: You should know this information in advance) to fill out the necessary paper work. Confirm the date and time with the new employee and close by stating: "Great (new employee's name), I look forward to seeing you. And again, we're excited about having you join our team!"

2. When the new employee arrives to the office the OPM or Office Manager will walk out to reception area to greet the applicant.

3. Be sure to firmly shake his/her hand and be genuinely excited to see him/her. Con-tinue by following outlined script:

   Office: (Employee name), it's nice to see you again. (Spend a couple of minutes in the reception area exchanging small talk about the weather, sports or any other topic you like.) (Employees name), let's go back to my office for a few moments so that I can tell you a bit more about your new job. Take employee to your office and start off by offering him/her a cup of coffee or a soft drink.

   Office: (Employee name), before we get started let me tell you that we feel like you are the ideal person for our team, for the following reasons:

   (Know the reasons in advance, i.e. has a great personality that should be excellent at making customer cheerleaders, past employers stated how good his/her abilities were at the previous job, etc.) Before I ask you to complete the required paperwork, allow me a couple of minutes to review your job description and benefits. At this time the manager will read each duty required of job description along with hours, lifting requirements, uniforms, pay dates, rate of pay, benefits, etc.

Office: (Employee name), do you have any questions about your new job, pay, benefits or any questions at all? Answer each question or concern honestly and firmly.

Office: (Employee name), now comes the paperwork. I have several forms and documents for you to read and sign. (Explain each form while handing over to employee and give a brief explanation of its purpose). I.e., this is a W-4 form required by the federal government.

This is our In Case Of Emergency Form that will give us a contact person, such as a spouse or family member, for use in the unlikely event that you were ever injured while on the job)etc.

4. As each form and document is signed, check the appropriate box on the Applicant to Employee status tracking form.

5. If uniforms are available for the new hire they will be issued at this time along with policies regarding use and care. And of course you will have him/her sign the uniform receipt and you will check it off on the tracking form.

6. Save the Employee Policy Manual for last. When time for manual handout you will have the new employee sign off on the receipt of manual form. Inform the employee of the importance of our policy manual and ask that he/she reads it completely through at their earliest convenience. And should they have any questions, assure them that we operate with an open door management style and they can feel free to speak to our management at any time.

7. After all forms and paperwork have been completed, inform the new employee of the start date and time. This is usually the following work date.

8. Before closing out the meeting, give the new team member a brief overview of the orientation and training program agenda.

9. Close the meeting with the following script:

Office: (Employee name), it appears as though we have taken care of all of the paperwork and as of right now you are officially a member of the (your company) family. On behalf of everyone at (your company) I want to once again thank you for choosing us for you place of employment and know that you will do very well with our company.

I look forward to seeing you at (time and date). So, if you have no further questions of me, I will see you then. Thank You!

Tracking Applicant to Employee Status

Purpose: To allow for an organized method by which to ensure that all applicants are checked for suitability before being considered for employment. Once employed, to ensure that new employees have filled out all required paper work and have received all of our orientation and training to give them a good foundation for working with your company.

Steps: Completing of the Employee tracking form will begin at the time a decision has been made to consider an applicant for employment. This form will be kept in the new employee's file and will have each line item checked off after the task has been completed.

❑ Received application

❑ Reference check complete

❑ Applicant Risk Detector test given (ARD) [] Interview completed

❑ Candidate scheduled for a physical and drug screen

❑ Received criminal records check

❑ Received results of physical and drug screen and forward to GM [] Applicant contacted—hired and given a start date for orientation

❑ New employee introduction to our Production and Management Team [] New Team Member given a tour of facility

❑ Make copy of driver's license

❑ Received and made a copy of liability insurance card.

Employee has completed required documentation

- ❏ I-9
- ❏ W-4 (State)
- ❏ W-4 (Federal)
- ❏ In case of emergency
- ❏ Proof of Insurance
- ❏ Employment agreement
- ❏ Signed for and received copy of the company policies
- ❏ Complete Orientation
- ❏ Issued uniforms
- ❏ OSHA and safety training
- ❏ Given a driver's skills test - production only
- ❏ Received first week evaluation meeting

Policy Manual

The following is a policy manual intended for your use as the basis for a policy manual that you can put in place at your business. While the basic 'bones' of this document should be ready to go, you will need to customize the manual based on your policies, procedures, etc. Each business is a little bit different, so you should spend a good deal of time thinking through your policies before putting the manual into use.

Why do you need a policy manual in the first place? The world is a complicated place, and business is even more complicated still. Almost from day one of running your business, issues are sure to come up that you will need to have answers for. In order to keep everyone on the same page during their employment with the company, a policy manual is the best way to go. The employee will be able to consult their copy of the manual for any questions they may have, and the business can point to the manual when an issue arises that an employee has a complaint about. For legal reasons, having a signed copy of the manual from each employee will give you peace of mind that everyone has accepted the terms and conditions of their employment with your business.

(Your Company)
POLICY MANUAL

The policies and procedures in this manual are not intended to be contractual commitments by (company name), or any of its divisions. And they shall not be construed as such by employees. Employees have the right to resign their employment any time, without notice, for any reason or no reason. Our company retains a similar right to discontinuation of the employment of any employee. No permanent employment or employment for any term is intended or can be implied from any statements in this manual.

The described policies, practices and procedures in this handbook are carried out at the sole discretion of (company name) and are subject to change at any time without notice. Any changes will be in writing and posted on the break room bulletin board until they can be permanently incorporated into the handbook. No officer, employee or agent of (company name), will be authorized to waive, modify, or add to any of the provisions in this handbook, without the express written consent to do so, by the president of (company name). Any decisions by the president as to the interpretation or application of its policies, practices and procedures will be final and binding on all employees concerned. The policies and procedures are intended to be guides to management and are merely descriptive of suggested procedures to be followed. (Company name) reserves the right to revoke, change or supplement guidelines at any time without notice. No policy is intended as a guarantee of continuity of benefits or rights. No permanent employment or employment for any term is intended or can be implied by any statements in this manual.

(Your Company)
(Your Address)

Revision Date: (Used any time changes are made)

Chapter 1	**Our Company**	

Section: Welcome Aboard Letter

Welcome To the (Your Company) Family!

LETTER FROM THE PRESIDENT

It is with great pleasure that I welcome you to the (your company) family!

I believe you are joining our company at an exciting time. The industry is changing and so is our company. To win, we are selecting those persons it is felt can take our company to the next level of success. I feel that you will be a great asset and will contribute much to our success.

As you work with our company you will find the work can be interesting and as challenging as you make it. Our expectations are high and employees have been selected who also have high expectations.

Finally, you will find that you work with professionals who have high expectations and are concerned about the success of their company. I feel that you will compliment your co-workers by the strengths you bring to our company. Each of our employees is valued for their contribution to our success.

To help you during your employment with (company name) we have prepared a handout of company policies, which you are asked to read. If you have any questions concerning any policies, please feel free to speak with your manager or his representative. Your understanding of these policies will help make your time with our company a pleasant one and help you succeed while you help push our company to the next level of success.

Once more, welcome to (company name)! (Your name) President

Acknowledged Receipt of Policy Manual 1000

I have received my copy of the (your company) Policy Manual, which outlines the policies, practices, and benefit guidelines of the company. I understand that it is my responsibility to read and understand the contents in this manual.

I agree to observe and follow all policies, practices and regulations in the manual.

This manual is property of (your company). I agree to return this manual in good condition upon my separation with company.

Employee's Signature _____Date ___/___/

Company History and Philosophy 1010

(Your company) was formed in (month and year). We offer a wide range of cleaning and restoration services to an area encompassing (your city or geographical area) of (your state).

(Your Services Listed)
Oriental and area rug cleaning
Drapery cleaning, In-plant and on location, water loss restoration and drying services, carpet and upholstery cleaning
Urine removal services

Fire damage restoration

Mold remediation

Re-build services

Thermal inspections (FLIR)

Consulting services

Company Philosophy

In every industry there is usually one company that stands above the rest as a symbol of quality and excellence. In the cleaning and restoration industry we are determined to be that company. We were formed on the time-honored principals of trust, hard work, superior quality, and excellent customer service. (Your own philosophy) Without our clients and employees we would have little reason to be in business. All the manuals, offices and equipment are simply worthless without our clients and you, our valued employee. At (company name) impeccable service to our clients is much more than just an idea, it is a way of life.

The whole philosophy of our company revolves around our ability to deliver a service that is so good that our customers will be delighted and will go out of their way to find us new customers. We call these delighted clients "cheerleaders."

We ask you to do whatever it takes to please our clients. We will never question your actions as long as we have a delighted client. Your advancement and earning potential with our company are directly connected with your relationship with our clients.

Commitment to Employees   1020

In addition to our clients, the management of this company realizes the importance of its employees. We realized long ago that without honest, reliable, hardworking, and caring employees we would stand little chance of fulfilling our business objectives as well as our vision. We need you! And we appreciate you. After all, you and the services you perform are all we have to sell.

It is the goal of our company to provide you with a secure, fulfilling career where you are treated with respect and dignity. We want you to look forward to coming to work and to view our company as a family. We believe that education is the most valuable tool that we can give to our team. As a member of our team we will give you all the training necessary to assist you in becoming the best that you can be.

Our company philosophy is to provide our employees with year-round employment and compensation that is unmatched for comparable work. Our company is poised for continued growth and we do want our employees to be a part of our exciting future. We encourage your questions and ideas.

Growth, Profit, and Business Plan   1030

Our company was formed with limited resources of less than (your start-up seed) in (your year formed). (If incorporated) Our company was incorporated in (month and year), and operates under all applicable corporate laws for the state of (your state).

Our growth as a company has continued to surpass the national average for similar service companies operating in markets of equal size as ours.

(Company name) has continued to operate profitably since (year).

Business Plan

Our business plan is an aggressive plan which will allow us to continue to gain market share for our services in (your area) through the end of (three-year plan) which our short term business plan covers.

(Add any other pertinent information regarding your plan here. This can be anything from plans to open another location or even diversification. Your employees will appreciate your willingness to share your plans with them.)

Continuity of Policies   1040

To preserve the ability to meet company needs under changing conditions, (your company) may modify, add, delete, or revoke any and all policies, procedures, practices, and statements contained in this manual at any time without notice.

Such changes shall be effective immediately upon approval by management; unless otherwise stated.

Equal Opportunity	2000
Recruitment	2010
Sexual Harassment	2020
Smoking	2030
Employee Safety	2040
Workers Compensation	2050

We Are A Team: Fair, Honest, and Supportive Of One Another!

Equal Opportunity   2000

Equal opportunity is (company name) policy. It is our policy to select the best-qualified person for each position in our company. No employee of the company will discriminate against an applicant for employment or a fellow employee because of race, creed, color, religion, sex, national origin, ancestry, age, or other physical or mental handicap, or because of a person's veteran status.

This policy applies to all employment practices and personnel actions.

Recruitment   2010

(Company name) provides equal opportunity to all applicants on the basis of demonstrated ability, experience and training. As positions become available within the company, prior to outside recruitment, the operations manager shall determine the availability of qualified candidates within the company. Recruitments may be conducted through newspapers, schools, employment agencies, employee referrals, and company advertising.

The company bulletin board will display all current openings.

Sexual Harassment   2020

It is the policy of (company name) to provide a work place that is free of sexual harassment. Employees are prohibited from making either directly or indirectly any gestures, comments, suggestions, or advances to another employee that could be interpreted as harassment while on duty.

Smoking   2030

Smoking is not allowed inside of, or on any job site at any time. Our facility is a smoke free environment. This policy is for the health and safety of all employees. Your cooperation is requested as this policy must be rigidly enforced to comply with the company health safety requirements and to maintain proper insurance coverage for our customers.

Employee Safety   2040

It is the intent of (company name) to provide each new employee the knowledge and tools necessary to work safely within the daily work environment.

The safety program of (company name) is implemented as follows:

Upon being hired into the company, a new employee is introduced to supplies and equipment commonly used by the company and is familiarized with the safety features, product makeup, and potential hazards of supplies and equipment.

During the training period new employees are trained on the proper application of commonly used chemicals and cleaning products. Proper use of equipment is also discussed. Employees are required to follow all safety instructions stated by product manufacturer and company management.

It is your right as an employee of this company to know the chemical makeup of cleaners used on a regular or infrequent basis. For the safety of all employees, (company name) has established a material data sheet (MSDS) resource center located in the employee break area.

As company adds new chemicals or cleaners to its line, new MSDS will be incorporated into the resource center.

Employees should seek out the assistance of their immediate supervisor or safety officer when unclear about MSDS concerns.

Worker's Compensation   2050

If you are injured or suffer an accident or illness that is work related, you are covered under the provisions of the Worker's Compensation Law. This compensation insurance provides sick pay and certain payments for medical treatment. Be sure to notify your immediate supervisor of an injury, as the law requires that we file a First Report of Injury form within 48 hours of the injury.

Employees with any permanent physical impairments should notify the operations manager of such impairment upon their hiring or upon the onset of such impairment so they are registered with the Worker's Compensation Commission.

The Worker's Compensation Insurance Authority also gives the employer purchasing the insurance the right to designate the medical provider for all employees. Should employees seek medical assistance from someone other than the designated medical provider, the employee may be responsible for the expense and fees incurred and may be denied any benefits to be paid by the WCIA.

Our company has a designated medical provider for all employees suffering an injury or an illness that is work related. At the time the injury is reported, you will be advised to seek medical attention from our designated medical provider. The office will immediately call and set up the visit for you.

Should the injury or illness require immediate attention and no one is available, you will be sent to the local hospital emergency room for emergency care until a member of the designated medical provider can arrive.

Should medical professionals outside our designated medical provider be required, the staff and doctors will refer you to the appropriate doctor, therapist, etc. The designated medical provider will furnish our company with documentation as to what modifications or suspensions of work must be made to assist the healing process. Whenever possible, our company will work with the staff of the designated medical provider to modify your workload should the need arise.

Employment Classifications   2060

The majority of positions within the company are generally designed to require full time employees. In certain functions and during some seasons, work schedules and company needs may require the services of other than full time employees. There are three classifications of employees at (company name):

Regular Part-Time: An employee hired for an indefinite period in a position for which the normal work schedule is at least 20 but less than 40 hours per week.

Temporary: An employee hired for a position for which the scheduled workweek can range from less than 20 to 40 hours, but the position is required for only a specific, known duration, usually less than six months.

Full-Time: An employee hired for an indefinite period in a position for which the normal work schedule will range from at least 40 but less than 50 hours per week.

If you are unclear as to your status, please contact Operations Manager.

Anniversary Date   2070

An employee's anniversary date is defined as his/her first day on the job with the company.

Reinstatement Date   2080

Employees who are re-employed by the company after termination or separation will lose their original anniversary date and be assigned a new date corresponding to their first day on the job after re-employment. This policy shall not apply to layoffs or to an employee who was erroneously terminated and later reinstated.

Relatives   2090

It is the policy of (company name) to consider the hiring of relatives of existing employees if they meet the requirements for accepting employment with the company. If relatives are hired, it is the responsibility for each member to have a reliable vehicle and not to be dependent upon his/her relative for transportation. This issue will be addressed on an individual basis, but at no time will a family member be retained if he/she disrupts the operation of the company by necessitating transportation for them during a scheduled workday.

Return to Work after Serious Injury   2100

As a joint protection to the employees and the company, employees who have been absent from work because of serious illness or injury are required to obtain a doctors release specifically stating that the employee is capable of performing his/her duties. A serious injury or illness is defined as one that results in the employee being absent from work for more than ten work days, or one which may limit the employees future work performance.

The management of (company name) will ensure that employees returning to work after serious injury or illness are physically capable of performing their duties without risk of re-injury. If cause of employee injury or illness was job related, the management of (company name) will make every reasonable effort to assign employee to assignments that are consistent with the instructions of the employee's doctor until the employee is fully recovered. A doctor's release is required before recovery can be assumed.

Performance Improvement   2110

Performance improvement may be suggested when company management believes that an employee's performance is less than satisfactory and can be resolved through adequate counseling. Corrective counseling is completely at the discretion of company management. (Company name) expressly reserves the right to discharge "at will." Even if corrective counseling is implemented, it may be terminated at the discretion of management. Management, in its sole discretion, may either warn, reassign, suspend, or discharge any employee at will; whichever it chooses, and at any time. The operations manager will determine the course of action best suited to the circumstances.

The Steps in Performance Improvement are as Follows:

Verbal Counseling: As the first step in correcting unacceptable performance or behavior, the immediate supervisor will review pertinent job requirements with the employee to ensure his/her understanding of them. The supervisor will consider the severity of the problem, the employee's previous behavior and performance and all of the circumstances surrounding the particular case. The supervisor will document the verbal counseling for future reference.

Written Counseling: If the unacceptable performance or behavior continues, the next step will be a written warning. Certain circumstances, such as violations of a widely known policy, may justify a written warning without using verbal counseling. The written warning defines the problem and how it may be corrected. A written warning will indicate that probation or termination or both, may result if improvement is not observed. Written counseling becomes a part of the employee's personnel file, although the supervisor may remove the warning after a period of time under appropriate circumstances.

Probation: If the problem has not been resolved through written counseling or, if the circumstances warrant it, or both, the employee may be placed on probation. Probation is a serious action in which the employee is advised that termination will occur if improvement in performance or conduct is not achieved within the probationary period. Disciplinary probation periods are at the sole discretion of the supervisor.

Termination   2120

Employment with (company name) is normally terminated through one of the following actions:

Resignation: An employee desiring to terminate employment, regardless of employee status, is expected to give as much advance notice as possible. Two weeks or ten working days is generally considered to be sufficient notice time.

Dismissal: An employee may be discharged if his/her performance is unacceptable. The operations manager shall have counseled the employee concerning performance deficiencies, provided direction for improvement, and warned the employee of possible termination if performance did not improve within a certain period of time.

Misconduct: An employee found to be engaged in activities such as, but not limited to: theft of company property, insubordination, conflict of interest, or any other activities showing willful disregard of company interest or policies will be terminated. Termination resulting from misconduct shall be entered into the employee's personnel file. The employee shall be provided a written summary of the reason for termination.

Layoff: When a reduction in work force is necessary, or one or more positions are eliminated, the company will in its sole discretion, identify the employees to be laid off. The company may give two weeks' notice to the employee, but it reserves the right to substitute two weeks' severance pay in lieu of notice. Such pay will be based on the average hours worked during the last workweek at the employee's regular rate of pay.

Chapter 3 Compensation	Section
Equal Pay	3000
Job Descriptions	3010
Compensations Policies	3020
Salary Ranges	3030
Salary Surveys	3040
Merit Increases	3050
Workday	3060
Payday	3070
Pay Advances	3080
Overtime Compensation	3090
Meal and Rest Periods	3100

Mileage Reimbursement	**3120**
Drive Time Pay	**3130**
Employee Incurred Expense-Reimbursement	**3140**
Performance Evaluations	**3150**
Training and Certification	**3160**
Time Cards	**3170**
Equal Pay	**3000**

(Company name) will not pay wages to any employee at a rate less than what the company pays employees of the opposite sex for comparable work requiring comparable skills, assuming that time in company is equal.

Job Descriptions   3010

(Company name) has established job descriptions for every position within the company. Job descriptions have been established to assist employees in better understanding their jobs and serves as a tool for management in evaluating employee performance.

Job descriptions are also used to compare our positions with the positions of other companies for salary surveys. Position descriptions are also one of the factors used in setting pay scale positions within our company.

Job Descriptions include the following components:

A brief overview of the position, describing its basic function and the role it plays within the rest of the company.

• A list of duties required of the position holder
• An explanation of the reporting structure for the position.
• Necessary qualifications required for the position.
• Training necessary.

JOB DESCRIPTION

PRESIDENT/CEO

• Sets the vision and direction of the company
• Sets annual departmental budgets
• Analyzes financial condition of company on a weekly basis
• Conducts evaluations of management

- Interviews and hires for management
- Training and overseeing management staff
- Trouble shooting external
- Trouble shooting internal
- Evaluate and approve work orders

PROJECT MANAGER (PM)

Reports to President

Supervision

- Supervise and monitor all production staff
- Make decisions on difficult scheduling problems

Water Damage

- Prepare billing report
- Schedule re-installs
- Schedule final cleaning
- Schedule sub contractors
- Schedule pack-out if necessary
- Liaison to client/adjuster

Commercial Carpet Cleaning

- Schedule regular work
- Schedule special work
- Maintain yearly/monthly schedule
- Maintain commercial key legend and file
- Prepare letters outlining work/schedule as needed
- Troubleshoot Employees

Hiring

- Review screened applicants
- Choose production applications for interviews
- Interview for production
- Hire for production
- Prepare weekly "condition" report for president

Financial

- Monitor financial conditions of company i.e. production, collections, cash flow and payables, etc.
- Prepare weekly "condition" report for president
- Preparing job budgets
- Submitting purchase orders
- Preparing departmental budgets
- Writing and enforcing contracts

Safety

- Maintain and update MSDS
- Check our chemicals to ensure proper labeling
- Check OSHA compliance
- Check to ensure compliance by all employees
- Administer safety related test on employees
- Maintain employee sign off safety log
- Develop and institute employee safety training programs
- Train all production employees

Employees Training Seminars

- Schedule outside training programs
- Schedule transportation, lodging, etc.
- Prepare itinerary
- Request monies needed for participants and arrange disbursements
- Review expense reports and make financial adjustments as needed

Manuals

- Write and maintain Project and Safety Manuals

DIRECTOR OF MARKETING (DOM)

Reports to President Trade Show Coordinator

- Scheduling: Times, employees and activities
- Advertising/printing/execution
- Booth management

Newsletter

- Compile (articles, pictures, etc.)
- Type information
- Arrange with printer/coordinate our mailing

Electronic Media

- Assist in developing copy for radio spots
- Prepare and submit to president any electronic media advertising proposals
- Confirm scheduling of radio programs

Newspaper/Direct Mail

- Assist with ad layout and design
- Ensure that we are operating within our allotted budget for advertising
- Maintain ongoing contact with our appointed newspaper advertising representative
- Schedule all advertising
- Update demographic changes in our operating areas as they become available
- Plan and supervise office assistant with direct mailings

Agents

- Personal visits with agents in our service area for the purpose of building relationships for referrals
- Inviting agents to our facility for continuing educational training
- Developing an agent profile - used internally

Adjusters

- Cold-calling claims adjusters to promote our services
- Taking adjusters to lunch for relationship building
- Inviting adjusters to our training classes

Training Seminars

- Schedule and arrange payment
- Schedule transportation, lodging, etc.
- Prepare itinerary
- Request monies needed for participants and arrange disbursements
- Review expense reports and make financial adjustments as needed

Manuals

• Write and maintain marketing manuals

Supervision

• Interview and hire field representatives
• Supervise and monitor all field representatives

Contracted Agencies

• Develop and maintain relationship with advertising agencies
• Request proposals from outside agencies as needed and budget cost out of marketing budget

Marketing Plan

• Develop and maintain marketing plan
• Develop competitive analysis
• Develop competitive strategies

RESTORATION SPECIALIST

Reports to Restoration Crew Chief/OPM/PM

Salary Range - (Your Hourly Wages or Salary)

Duties

• Filling out work orders
• Inspecting carpet, furniture, and draperies prior to cleaning
• Carpet cleaning
• Upholstery cleaning
• Drapery cleaning
• Pet urine inspections/removal services
• Truck/Equipment maintenance
• Measuring carpet
• In plant cleaning of rugs, miscellaneous items
• Spot/stain removal services
• Writing receipts for cash, credit cards, and checks
• Adding value in the home
• Up selling of products and services
• Maintain your assigned equipment/toolbox

- Communicating with our customers
- Making customer cheerleaders
- Water loss restoration
- Demolition
- Smoke and soot removal

RESTORATION CREW CHIEF

Reports to OPM/PM

Salary Range—(Your Hourly Wages or Salary)

Duties

- Filling out work orders
- Inspecting carpet, furniture, and draperies prior to cleaning

Carpet cleaning

- Managing work crews in house and temporary contracted
- Assisting in scoping and estimating of job sites
- Training of restoration specialist
- Training of temporary and contracted labor force
- Upholstery cleaning
- Drapery cleaning
- Pet urine inspections/removal services
- Truck/Equipment maintenance
- Measuring carpet
- In plant cleaning of rugs, miscellaneous items
- Spot/stain removal services
- Writing receipts for cash, credit cards, and checks
- Adding value in the home
- Up selling of products and services
- Maintain your assigned equipment/toolbox
- Communicating with our customers
- Making customer cheerleaders
- Water loss restoration
- Demolition
- Smoke and soot removal

OFFICE MANAGER (OM)

Salary

Reports to Operations Manager/President Applications

- Do reference checks as needed and report results to OM or President

Mail

- Distribute company mail

Telephone

- Answer telephone as needed

Employee Files/Payroll

- Keep all employee files current
- Former employees – keep records of
- Review daily time sheets for accuracy – for both regular employees and temp help
- Keep track of all sick days and vacation days
- Simple IRA retirement plan – manage company retirement plan
- Prepare bi-monthly payroll for all employees
- Pay monthly tax deposits
- Prepare monthly and quarterly payroll forms and filing
- Prepare yearly 940 and W-2's as required

Insurance & Taxes

- Maintain all required insurance policies and update as necessary
- Responsible in ensuring proper filing of tax return for company
- Yearly renewal of corporation and dues filing

Filing

- Expenses - keep record of all expenses for all departments
- Deposits - keep records of all deposits made

Computer Back-Up-(This includes all Computers in Office)

- Back up BBS daily
- Quicken/QuickBooks – monthly
- Entire System – bi-monthly trouble-shoot network problems company web-site
- Keep information on web-site current

- Insert all upcoming company CE classes on insurance page of web-site for registration

Purchases

- Approve all P.O. relating to retail and service supplies

WDR/FDR JOBS

- Create job folders
- Verify all job info for accuracy
- Produce accounting system budget for all ongoing jobs
- Determine responsible party for payment
- Get mortgage information when necessary (for payment)
- Prepare variance reports comparing budget and actual for labor/materials (original budget prepared by estimator)
- Load all job photos onto network (computer)
- Submit all billing for jobs
- Close jobs in Exactimate and JPP (Job Processing Program) when completed
- Maintain files on all ongoing jobs
- Maintain files on all completed jobs
- Reports on sales for WDR/FDR

Invoicing/Accounts Receivable/Collections

- Prepare invoicing for all jobs and mail out-computer entry and billing
- Send follow up letters for unpaid invoices
- Make quality check calls as needed
- Make contact with person responsible for payment of services (i.e. insured, home-owner, agent or adjuster)
- Apply finance charges for overdue accounts and mail out
- File in small claims for collection on accounts past 90 days
- Refer accounts to collection agency used by company after 90 days of non-payment
- Credit all payments that are received
- Prepare deposits for bank (deposits are made by OA.)

Accounts Payable

- Pay all bills
- Maintain all accounts that are on credit

Continuing Education

• Schedule classes for continuing education as requested by president

CE Classes

• Assist marketing director in preparation
• Keep CE classes current with the state

OFFICE ASSISTANT (OA)

Reports to Office Manager

Salary — (Your Hourly Wages or Salary)

Phone Duties

• For phone 8:00 a.m. – 5:00 p.m.

Typing as Needed

• Misc. correspondence (letters, procedures, estimates, etc.)
• Commercial work "quotes"

Applications

• Take applications
• Maintain application file
• Screen applications (per request only)
• Do reference checks (per request)
• Submit possible applicants to supervisor for review
• Set up interviews (per request)
• Send out rejection letters

Manuals

• Maintain parts/equipment manuals
• Maintain employee manual
• Maintain operations manual

Prepare Folders

• Residential and commercial inspections
• Commercial inspections
• Residential and commercial jobs
• In plant

- Water and fire damage

Minutes of Company Meetings

- Take minutes
- Maintain notebook and computer file w/minutes
- Distribute at next meeting
- Assist in agenda preparation when necessary

Errands

- Bank deposits
- Pickup and delivery of keys
- Purchase supplies as directed
- Pickup donuts for company functions

Mail

- Sort mail and distribute
- Prepare outgoing mail
- Prepare sort and deliver bulk mail
- Prepare shipment and arrange deliveries

Filing Duties

- Residential
- Commercial
- Restoration
- Customer files
- Daily work orders
- Accounts payable/receivable
- Payment records
- Brochure/literature files
- Prepare billings
- Set up new files
- Folder information
- Credit plus sales

Thank You Notes

- For carpet cleaning jobs

- For one-time house cleanings
- For in-plant cleaning
- For referrals
- For inspections given

Reminder Letters/Cards

- Send out stock reminder cards and letters monthly calendar work
- Enter scheduled jobs daily onto calendar
- Crosscheck calendar daily against computer schedule

Computer Back-Up

- Back-up BBS daily
- Back-up Quicken monthly
- Back-up entire system bi-monthly

Key Issuing and Return of Keys

- Issue keys to all employees each day
- Ensure safe return of all keys each day
- Maintain key assignment sheet

OFFICE ASSISTANT- BOOKKEEPING DUTIES

Processing Work Orders

- Enter work orders in computer
- Print out invoices for unpaid customers
- Follow up on any notes left by crews
- Check in key: Return to box/return to client
- Make quality check calls:
- Copies of positive comments to crew and manager
- Schedule re-cleans
- Put copy of quality control check forms in managers basket
- Send paperwork through for approval

Processing Work Orders (completed)

- Carpet
- Process and distribute copies of day sheets
- Enter jobs into computer

- Follow up on any notes left by crew manager
- Schedule re-cleans
- Put copy in crews' basket
- Put copy in managers basket (quality control check forms)
- Send paperwork through for approval
- Maintain restoration log

Accounts Receivable (assist Office Manager)

- Review day sheets for adjustments
- Review work orders for adjustment
- Send through for computer entry and billing

Daily Time Sheets (for payroll)

- Time card preparation
- List sell-ups, commissions, and bonuses, etc.
- Verify with day sheets/work orders before forwarding to OM

Prepare Bank Deposits

- Sort checks by residential/commercial
- Make up deposit
- Maintain petty cash and journal

Accounts Payable

- Review Accounts payable
- Send through for computer entry
- Make copies of all receipts in AP slot and file

Workers Compensation

- Maintain file-active, inactive
- File 1st report of injury
- File all papers necessary
- Supply medical provider with information
- Get release for work or discuss modification
- Track employee improvement

Collections (assist OM)

- Monitor receivables

- Send out reminders
- Make collection calls on daily basis
- File small claims as required

Compensation Policies   3020

It is important that each employee of (company name) understand the company's compensation policies and procedures.

Compensation Objectives:

(Company name) wants each employee to be paid compensation that:

- Rewards good performance
- Fairly reflects the duties and responsibilities of each position
- Will attract, motivate, and retain competent persons
- Is cost effective for the company

Salary Ranges   3030

Each job is assigned a specific salary grade. Frequently more than one job will be in a particular grade. The salary range represents the "going rate" in the marketplace for trained, experienced employees.

Each salary grade will have a minimum, mid-point, and maximum salary for all positions in that grade. The minimum salary is a fair rate for a person who just meets the basic qualifications of a job, with little or no experience. The mid-point of the salary range is considered an appropriate rate of pay for an experienced, fully qualified, competent employee performing all duties and responsibilities of the position in a completely satisfactory manner. The maximum of the salary range is the upper limit of the potential dollar value a position is worth to (company name). Each employee will be informed of his/her salary grade and the range for the grade.

At the discretion of the department manager an employee may be paid a salary over and above the maximum salary range if he/she has demonstrated an ability to perform to high standards. The easiest and best way to max out a salary range is to make lots of "Customer Cheerleaders."

POSITION	MINIMUM	MID-RANGE	MAXIMUM
Restoration Specialist	$	$	$
Restoration Crew Chief	$	$	$
Office Assistant	$	$	$
Operations Manager	Salary		
Director Of Marketing	Salary		
Accounts Manager	Salary		
Office Manager	Salary		
Project Manager	Salary		
Production Manager	Salary		
Carpenter	$	$	$
Lead Carpenter	$	$	$

Salary Surveys   3040

To ensure that (company name) salary ranges are competitive with companies of comparable size in similar business, (company name) will conduct periodic salary surveys. The (position holder) of (company name) will review the results of these surveys. Salary ranges will be adjusted when necessary to remain competitive.

Merit Increases   3050

Annually, the president of (company name) will approve a budget for merit salary increases. The operations manager will determine if a merit increase is warranted at the time of the performances evaluation. It is (company name) policy to reward employees with merit increases in salary for dedication in their work, extra effort and better than average performance.

Management does not award merit increases on an automatic basis or at any preset interval. All approved merit increases will be made retroactive to the first workday of the week of the performance evaluation.

Information pertaining to rates of pay and merit increases in pay are deemed to be confidential matters between the company and each employee and are not to be discussed among employees.

Workday   3060

A workday begins at the normal start time of 8 a.m., or unless a special time has been ordered by the operations manager. Time ends upon return to the office after the last scheduled job has been completed.

Specific workday and workweek hours for each employee will be determined from time to time based on the operational needs of the company. (Company name) will attempt to notify employees of any changes in start or finish times as much advance notice as possible.

Payday   3070

The company paydays are on the 15th and 30th of each month. For paydays that fall during a weekend, checks will be distributed on the Monday following the payday. If a company holiday falls on the 15th or 30th, employees will receive their paycheck on the last workday prior to the holiday.

Pay is issued after 11 a.m. on paydays. Employees who have resigned from company without proper notice will not be allowed to pick up paycheck at office. Employees who resign without the required proper notice will have pay sent out through postal service to the place of their residence as was listed on their employment application.

Pay Advances   3080

It is company policy to decline all requests for early paychecks or pay advances. Pay advances in the event of emergency reasons may be requested through the operations manager. Employee requesting an emergency pay advance or early paycheck must provide evidence of such a need.

Overtime Compensation   3090

Employees will be paid at a rate of one and one half times their regular rate of pay for the following:

• Hours worked in excess of 40 in a single workweek.
• Hours worked on a company holiday.
• Salaried employees are exempt from overtime status.

Meal and Rest Periods   3100

Meal Period – Employees are permitted one hour each day for a non-paid lunch break. Lunch breaks should be taken between either the longest drive time of their work schedule or between the second or third job. The times for these drive time lunch breaks are to be taken at a time convenient with scheduling needs. Lunch is not to be taken in addition to drive time periods. Company does not pay for lunch breaks. Operations manager will assign lunch periods during the day if there is any conflict with scheduling. An automatic deduction of thirty minutes is taken daily for the lunch period, whether taken or not.

Mileage Reimbursement

When an employee uses his/her own vehicle for company business, that employee shall be reimbursed for company related business travel at the rate of (your rate) cents per mile.

Mileage reimbursement is paid out on regular paydays.

Travel expenses between your home and company office are not reimbursable.

Employees are responsible for making mileage entries on daily work orders and forwarding this information to operations manager upon completion of days' work.

Drive Time Pay   3120

Employees are paid for drive time during normal work hours. Such time is considered to be the safest, but most direct route to the job as described on the work order. In the event a member elects to take a route not described on the work sheet for a job, the member will only be paid for that amount considered by AERODRY accounting department to be the maximum allowable time to get to an assignment. Further, drive time is a paid event and is a benefit offered to AERODRY employees to compensate them for down time traveling from one work site to another.

Company is not responsible for traffic violations or any accident that would occur during any working hours.

Employee-Incurred Expense and Reimbursement   3130

To ensure that all proper business–related expenses incurred by employees are reimbursed, the following procedures have been established:

• All expenditures are to be approved in advance by the OM unless circumstances prevent advance notice. All business-related expenditures must be accompanied by a receipt or evidence of expenditure in order to receive reimbursement.

• Reimbursement will be made within five working days from date of expenditure.

Employee Performance Evaluations   3140

All production employees of company will be evaluated orally by the PM. The OM will orally evaluate all office staff. Production employee and staff oral evaluations will be followed up by written statement concerning employees evaluated and the actions to be taken.

Formal evaluations will be at 30 days, 90 days and at six months after start of employment. During the first two years of employment, a six-month formal evaluation schedule will be maintained. After two years with company, formal evaluation will be scheduled annually, unless a problem arises and needs to be addressed.

The department manager will discuss your performance evaluation with you. This is an opportunity for an assessment of your strengths and weaknesses. We also set goals for the future. Your evaluation does not imply that a raise or salary adjustment if forthcoming, however, salary increases as they apply to your performance will be considered. Your salary is based upon the requirements of your job in terms of skill, education, experience and responsibility. To a large degree your salary will be based on how well you are able to make ("Customer Cheerleaders")

Each Employee will be rated from one of the following:

O. Outstanding

Optimum performance in meeting every basic position responsibility. A person in this category has comprehensive knowledge about his/her field and is highly experienced. This person achieves significantly more in quality and quantity than other employees. An individual in this category represents outstanding worth to (company name) in his/her position. This person requires minimal direction.

E. Excellent

This employee frequently exceeds the basic position requirements on some of the most difficult parts of the job. He/she in most cases achieves goals in a timely manner. This person requires little supervision. This individual frequently contributes a "little extra" and anticipates and takes appropriate action.

G. Good

This employee is performing all basic position responsibilities in an acceptable manner. The performance level is that expected of a qualified trained individual in the assigned position. Most work is completed on schedule. This person requires normal supervision and direction.

M. Marginal

A person in this category is not performing some of the basic responsibilities of the position in a satisfactory manner and frequently misses deadlines. Frequent and close supervision from immediate supervisor is required.

U. Unsatisfactory

A person in this category is failing to meet many basic position responsibilities and/ or is particularly deficient in one more of them.

Payroll Deductions   3150

The following mandatory deductions will be made from every employee's gross wages: federal income tax, social security FICA tax, and applicable city and state taxes.

Every employee must fill out and sign a federal and state with holding allowance certificate, IRS Form W-4, on his/her first day on the job. These forms must be completed in accordance with federal regulations. Employees may fill out a new W-4 at any time when his/her circumstances change.

Every employee will receive an annual Wage and tax statement, IRS Form W-2, for the preceding year on or before January 31. Any employee, who believes that his/her deductions are incorrect for any pay period, or on Form W-2, should check with accounts manager immediately.

Training and Certification   3160

One of the most important facets of our company is our employee. To this end we want to help you be the absolutely best at what you do. The old adage "the more you learn the more you earn" is very true. We really do want to help you advance and become professional.

Our Employee training program is instituted as follows:

Staff meetings – During meetings, training is given.

Formal Training – Training officer will conduct brief daily skills review with each new employee at the end of each work shift. A training officer will be assigned to you and will serve as your mentor and will assist you for the first two weeks with the company.

On the Job – During your initial 90-day probationary period, you will be paired with different experienced crew chiefs. The purpose of this is to give you hands-on experience that is taught by our own in-house experts. We think our crew chiefs are the best trainers that a company can have, but if you ever feel like you are not learning, please let the operations manager know so corrective action can be taken.

Video Tapes, audio cassettes, books and magazines are used during our ongoing training program. (Company name) has procured an extensive library of training aids. In addition, we will be developing our own in house training tapes and literature as needed.

Professional Seminars – Occasionally company will send selected employees to industry related seminars. Our seminar training programs are fully paid. When seminar sponsors offer testing, we will generally require the attending employee to test and will therefore expect our representative to be a high scorer.

In-House Seminars – Periodically our company sponsors in house speakers and you will be paid to attend. These events are very expensive, in both sponsor fees and lost production time, so please pay extra attention.

Good Housekeeping

Keeping work areas orderly and clean helps create a pleasant working atmosphere and is important in preventing injury. We want you to acquire good habits of cleaning your work area and equipment when the workday is over. Always exercise caution with items that could cause injury. PUT EVERYTHING IN ITS PROPER PLACE!

Integrity

Absolute honesty is a primary requirement in our business. Our customers entrust us with their money and other property because of their confidence in our company and the people who work for us. You are expected to conduct yourself and perform your job in a manner that deserves this trust at all times. Any proven acts of dishonesty will result in immediate dismissal. In addition this company will go to any length to protect our customer's interest. We will prosecute any employee for any illegal acts.

Your work orders are considered your time card and must be filled out correctly with your starting and leaving times for each job noted. Proceed directly to your next job! False reporting on a work order is grounds for immediate termination.

Chapter 4 Employee Benefits	Section
Vacation	4000
Holidays	4010
Professional Memberships	4020
Educational Assistance	4030
Service Awards	4040
Paid Sick Time	4050
Retirement Program	4060

Benefits, The Key To Your Personal Growth

Vacations 4000

To be eligible for vacation, employee must be available for work Monday through Friday from 8 a.m.-5 p.m. Vacation benefits are based on the employees' anniversary date. The schedule for vacation is as follows:

Anniversary Date in Calendar Year

1st through 2nd
3rd through 4th
5th or more

Vacation Entitlement

1 Week

2 Weeks

3 Weeks

New employees will be eligible for vacation days after one year's continuous employment with company. Employees leaving employment prior to the completion of one year of service will not receive any compensation for vacation days.

Company pays vacations. Paid vacations are figured at the employees' current rate of pay and at the average number of hours worked per week during the previous month. The employee's anniversary date is established according to the policy in Section 2070. To be eligible to take vacation, the employee must be in an active pay status. Vacation is not vested and terminated employee will not be paid for vacation not taken. The OPM is responsible for scheduling vacations. Normally, two weeks advance notice of vacation is expected and necessary to ensure adequate time to adjust company schedule.

Holidays   4010

The offices of (company name) are closed the following days: Christmas, New Year's Day, Memorial Day, Easter, Independence Day, Labor Day, and Thanksgiving. Unless a paid holiday is expressly given to an employee as a part of their employment package there are no company paid holidays.

Professional Memberships   4020

(Company name) encourages employees to become active in the many associations and organizations in the cleaning industry.

Employees who desire to become members in industry organizations may be eligible to receive up to 100% of membership dues. Employees interested in membership programs shall obtain information and authorization of operations manager.

Educational Assistance   4030

Employees are encouraged to further their knowledge of the industry. Company will pay up to 75% of educational cost for employees who voluntarily seek out further education. Company will pay 100% of cost for employees who are designated by management to receive further education.

Service Award   4040

(Company name) is committed to rewarding those employees that perform above average and go the extra mile for our customers and the company. On occasion, management will single out employees who have demonstrated above average behavior or work and will reward him/her with a complimentary bonus.

Awards are based on the following:
- Attendance
- Overall work performance
- Attitude
- Your ability to make "Customer Cheerleaders"

Paid Sick Time   4050

Company will provide (your sick time allowance) sick time per month for all full-time production personnel. To be eligible for sick time an employee must work a minimum of 35 hours per workweek. Sick time is computed at the close of each pay period.

Company has established a voluntary retirement program for those employees' interested in providing for their future. With this program company will contribute up to 3% of employee's annual salary into an IRA vehicle chosen by the employee. For more information regarding enrollment details please see the accounts manager.

Accounting

Generally speaking, most business owners loathe the accounting side of business and for good reason too! Entrepreneur's specialize in "dream weaving" and would rather be doing anything other than looking over the books and keeping track of all the nickels and dimes. When you ask an entrepreneur to ruminate on the early days when he first had the "vision" for his adventure, rarely will one admit that he fancied himself sitting behind a desk counting beans. With that said, a well-organized accounting process is key to your success, both in the short and long term. In fact, there is a strong correlation between businesses that fail and a lack of sound accounting practices with that failed business. Most cleaning and restoration businesses do not have to employ, nor should you retain the likes of the defunct Arthur Anderson for keeping books. QuickBooks by Intuit.com is a tremendous bookkeeping and payroll platform for cleaning and restoration operators. It's very affordable, easy to use, and once set up it will put much of the nitty-gritty accounting work on auto pilot.

There are numerous ways in which you can establish your accounts department. Whichever method you choose, you must have a system that ensures accountability for both the money brought into the business, as well as the money that flows out of the business.

In larger firms the receivables and payables duties are performed by separate individuals. The obvious reason for this structure is to lessen the possibility of an employee pilfering money from the company coffers. Before accusing me of believing that all employees will steal when given the chance, let me share my true opinion on the subject.

I wholeheartedly believe that the vast majority of human beings are honest and caring people. Having said that, I'd also state that there are some individuals who by any measure are hard working, caring and honest, but will steal if given the opportunity.

We've all heard the nightmare type stories about the people who went undetected for years stealing sometimes hundreds of thousands of dollars from the company's that they worked for and were entrusted with the companies check book.

Regardless of how smart of a business owner you are, or how popular and respected of an employer you believe yourself to be, especially in regards to your employees, you place your business at great risk without a system that has checks and balance mechanisms built in.

Having an unqualified individual handle your receivables and payables can at times be just as bad as having a thief handling your money, in that they are careless with your hard earned money.

For the smaller operator who cannot afford outside assistance from an accounting or bookkeeping firm, he must still have control over the revenues. Many startup businesses will enlist the help of their wife or husband to manage the books. If at all possible the spouse should not assume the position of accounts manager unless she or he is qualified.

Having a system of checks and balances only works if all members of your team understand that you have these security measures in place. I'll share a story that I believe best illustrates the point of what I'm hoping to get across.

Our service company had implemented a detailed system of utilizing purchase orders for any and all items purchased by our company. We got the word out to everyone in the company that all employees, myself included, were required to follow our purchase order procedures prior to making any purchase.

A couple of years after the procedures were instituted we became extremely busy. Within a period of one month we picked up over one million dollars in fire damage restoration work, much of which involved rebuild work. Subsequent to that the unthinkable happened. Here we were, busier than all get out, and the last thing I worried about was taking the time to fill out those trivial purchase orders. My employees recognized that due to the increased workload I had suddenly relaxed our security procedures regarding accountability for money leaving the business.

My project manager at the time was a good ole boy who loved to boast to anyone and everyone within ear shot about how honest of a man he was. With his glib tongue and the skills of a masterful illusionist, he was successful in discovering a hole the size of Texas in what we had believed was a foolproof system He magically pulled out several thousand dollars, as easy as a carnival magician pulls the rabbit out of his hat.

As a full service restoration operator you will be involved in the repair and rebuilding of structures damaged by fires, floods, tornadoes and many other type of calamity's. You will establish accounts with many lumberyards throughout your service area. These are great arrangements to work out due to the fact that you can set up the billing cycle on a net 30-day system. Returning to the story of Marvin the Magician. As it turned out he had concocted a system in which to steal several thousands of dollars from our company. One of the stores we have accounts with is Lowe's. This project manager, along with our lead carpenter, are issued Lowes cards under our company name.

This guy would purchase materials in two sets. One for the company and one for him. He and his accomplice, who happened to be one of his subordinates, would make the purchase, walk out one door of the store and then right back in the other door with returns on the duplicate materials. He would ask the clerk to put the return on a gift card as opposed to crediting our company account. Gift cards worked in this case because they were not traceable.

He would use the gift cards to purchase tools for himself, or he would sell the cards to the highest bidder.

How the scheme worked so well was that as the project manager, he was the individual who determined what materials were needed for a project. As such he was able to exaggerate the materials needed. As busy as we were at the time, we had no way of comprehending that he was ordering more materials than were called for on specific projects.

By now you may be wondering how his odyssey ended.

I stopped into the local Lowe's store and just happened to run across one of the girls I happened to know who works in the paint department. During casual discussion she inquired if we had a large bathroom remodel project underway. I expressed to her that we were in fact working a six-plex fire that had a total of twelve bathrooms being completely redone. She then asked what the rest of the shower units were being used for. According to her, she had seen my guys in the store earlier that day with a caravan of loaded carts reminiscent of a group of Amish men headed to a barn raising. Clearly that raised the proverbial red flag. So I proceeded to the customer service desk to inquire about the purchase. Lo and behold, there had been sixteen shower units charged to my account earlier that day.

Being the credulous guy I am, I'm thinking maybe I have mistaken the number of showers needed on this particular job. So I went to the job site and recounted the bathrooms and once again there are only two bathrooms per apartment, equaling a total of twelve shower units needed for this project.

This one incident of theft alone was valued in excess of $1,200.

As this story demonstrates—a system of accountability is a must for a cleaning and restoration business. Below are just a few of the other areas of your operation that must be made accountable:

• Opening of incoming mail. This is the way in which the majority of money flows into a business like ours.
• Preparing and making deposits.
• Posting of payments received—Income.
• Payment of bills—Accounts payable.
• Collections

The ideal process would be to have a bookkeeper do your accounts payables, payment of bills and payroll. Our bookkeeper comes in on a regular scheduled basis and is for the most part under lock and key to prevent the forming of relationships with other team members.

The procedures used in your business might look similar to this:

Step 1. The Office Assistant will collect incoming mail from the mailbox.

Step 2. The receptionist will put all mail in the Account Manager's mail slot.

Step 3. The Account Manager will distribute all mail to office personnel.

Step 4. Account Manager will credit all payments that were received into company's accounting software.

Step 5. After checks are credited they will be given to the receptionist for deposit. Checks are deposited two to three times weekly, depending, of course, on how much is coming in on a daily and weekly basis.

Step 6. Any bills that have come in for payment must be matched up with the appropriate Purchase Orders and filed for payment by due date.

Step 7. The person responsible for paying and processing payroll will do this on the 15th and the last workday of each month. Any additional payments that are needed throughout the month must be approved before they can be paid.

Collection of Payments for Services Rendered

One of the most important things in business is being able to collect for the services that you provide. If you go through all the trouble and expense of completing a job and fail to get paid, you will eventually wish that you were not in business.

Law of accounting 101. You cannot make a profit if you don't collect on each and every job.

Having a precise schedule for collecting is very important and must be monitored closely. We utilize several methods for collecting payment;

• Invoicing
• Telephone contact
• Small claims
• Collection agencies
• Attorneys

Attorneys are generally not needed that often, and then only in cases where a contract has been breached on a larger amount in excess of $5,000. The cleaning and restoration industry is blessed to have Mr. Ed Cross, also known as the restoration industry attorney, represent restoration owners in matters of collections, breach of contract, etc.

I would highly recommend that start–ups and industry veterans alike seek out Ed Cross for legal assistance. He has written nearly every type of legal document that a cleaning and restoration business will need during their business career. Tell Ed that Ivan sent you! <u>A sagacious friend once told me that it is smarter to be pro-active and plan ahead for success—versus being reactionary and getting caught with your pants down.</u>

An important consideration to keep in mind is that all the appropriate paperwork must be completed prior to commencing work on projects. This is where Ed Cross has you covered. A few examples are;

• Contracts
• Change orders

- Tradesman agreements
- Work authorizations
- Direction of payment
- Mechanics liens

When dealing with larger losses, you will have stated in your contract exactly how and when payment is expected to be rendered. We refer to these payments as progressives. This is where you spell out exactly how payment is to be made. An example may be that 33 percent is due at time of contract signing, 33 percent at the midway point of a job as defined by you, and the balance due in full on the signing on the certificate of completion. This information is all clearly spelled out in your contract.

Earlier, I emphasized the importance of always maintaining leverage on any and all jobs performed by your company. Here is an example; you begin a job without collecting the monies owed as were clearly spelled out in your contract. Another example would be to get to the half way mark and continue working without the money that is rightfully owed to you.

The next business day after a project has been completed, an invoice for our services is sent to the customer for the total amount due. It is a sound business practice to keep the billing cycle as short lived as possible. The longer you take to initiate the collection process, the less likely you will be of getting paid in full.

As a rule we do not bill for carpet cleaning services. This is something that we let our customers know in advance. We simply inform them that payment is expected upon completion of services. We also accept credit cards for their convenience. When a customer does not have cash or check, they may pay by credit card. We have found that as an added benefit of providing credit card availability, our typical customer often times spend more on add-on sales like Scotchgard, upholstery cleaning, drapery cleaning, etc. You get the point.

After the service has been completed and the credit card transaction completed, the office assistant will print out a computerized receipt, this receipt is mailed to the customer along with the itemized receipt for the services that were performed.

Step 1. After a job is completed the accounts manager is notified that all necessary paperwork is completed and that all tasks have been accomplished.

Step 2. Account manager will create an invoice for the total amount due (using Quick-

Books). All invoices have the notation that they are due upon receipt and that a mechanics lien will be placed if payment is not received within 30 days.

Step 3. The invoice will then be printed out in duplicate. One copy will go into the customer file and the other one will be sent out through the mail.

Step 4. A certificate of completion if (applicable) will be faxed or mailed to the adjuster and agent involved. A copy of the invoice, a copy of the direct payment authorization, and a copy of the estimate will be sent to the adjuster.

See samples in the appendix.

Step 5. If, after two weeks, nothing is heard, the account manager will call the adjuster in charge to find out if payment has been issued. If payment has been made to the insured, the account manager will contact the insured to find out about getting paid.

The following telescript is followed:

AERODRY; Hello Mr./Mrs. (customers name). This is (account manager's name) with (company's name), I am calling in regards to the Taylor Jones loss. The work at their home was completed on (date), and I am calling today to find out if payment has been made.

ADJUSTER: As a matter of fact, I just sent that out yesterday, and it will be coming directly to you. You should have it in a couple of days at most. (In this case, you will not need to do anything further).

Or:

ADJUSTER: We mailed the payment to the insured two weeks ago.

AERODRY: Was our name included on the check?

ADJUSTER: Yes, it was—In this case you know that the insured cannot deposit the check because it requires the endorsement of everyone listed on the check, or if adjuster answers no, your name is not on the check. In this case, you may have your work cut out for you. In most cases after calling your client you will be able to get full payment.

In some cases, this is the time that the opportunistic customer may accuse you of either not doing something that was on the estimate, or overcharging them for your services and demand a thorough explanation of your charges. In some cases they may just outright say that they are not going to pay the amount, maybe because they could have done it for less.

Step 6. If payment has not been received within 30 days, a phone call is made to the insured letting them know that we need to be paid. In addition, a letter stating that we will be forced to place a mechanics lien on their property and/or file a claim against them, in addition to forwarding all information to the credit bureau. This letter will give them a date that specifies when the action to collect will be carried out. Along with the letter we also send them a copy of the original invoice and a statement for the total amount due (including late fees). Late charges are assessed if payment is over 30 days past due.

This is usually fifteen days from the date of the letter, which gives them ample time to pay. (This is also the date of filing the mechanics lien).

Telephone script for calling the customer:

AERODRY: Hello Mrs. Jones, this is Lisa with AERODRY. I am calling regarding payment that we performed in your home back in May, 2006.

CUSTOMER: Yes?

AERODRY: We have not received payment, and would like to get your account closed. Is there a possibility that you could get the payment in the amount of (amount due with late fees) in the mail today? Or if it's easier perhaps you can drop it off at our office. I can waive the late fees that have already been assessed, however, if payment isn't received within three days, this offer will longer be available.

CUSTOMER: I will get it in the mail to you right away.

AERODRY: Thank you, Mrs. Jones, I will be looking for the payment then, by (date). Proceed as stated in step 6 to send out the letter explaining what will happen if we do not receive payment.

Step 7. If all collection efforts have failed at this point, we will proceed with filing a small claims judgment against them. If the small claims case is found in our favor we will then place a lien against their property (this is only if we haven't been paid at this point). If, after filing the small claims petition, the customer pays in full, we would then send/fax over a form (satisfaction of judgment) to the Small Claims Division showing that the judgment has been paid in full.

Step 8. If, after 60 days of judgment (in our favor), we have still not received payment, we would then turn all information over to a collection agency. The one that we use, charges 25% of the total payment made. They do not charge any fees if they do not collect.

Step 9. If, after 120 days, we still have not received payment and this claim is over $5,000, we would contact an attorney. The attorney would send a letter to client explaining our intent to take this case to court if not settled promptly. Before you decide to hire an attorney, you should first take into consideration the cost involved in doing so. Will it cost you $500, $1,000, $2,000, or even more? Even after all of these costs that you incur, will you be able to collect? I'm not saying that you should not attempt to go this route; I am just suggesting ask yourself some important questions:

1. Do I have a contract spelling out all terms and conditions of the work that was completed?

2. Did I have the customer sign a work authorization from the very beginning?

3. Did I take care of all problems or issues that the customer had? (Did my company personally go out and do a final punch list with the customer after the job was complete, and then take care of any problems pointed out by the customer?

4. Does the customer have any legitimate complaints at the present time that I have not addressed?

5. If you answered yes to all of the above, you probably have a pretty good case. If not, however, you may need to make some changes in your company to ensure that you will always be paid, even if you have to pursue it with the help of an attorney through no fault of your own. Face it, some people just do not want to pay their bill when the job is complete, even if you did everything right.

For a comprehensive administrative program designed specifically for the cleaning and restoration industry visit; showmemarketingsolutions.com.

Insurance

While it shouldn't occupy as much of your time or attention as human resources and accounting, business insurance is a vital part of your operation. You need to know what kinds of coverage to have, how much it should cost you, and how your policy needs change as your business grows and adapts. The following few pages are meant to give you a nice introduction to the world of business insurance and get you thinking about how your operation will need to be insured.

The Importance of Insurance

The most important rule of order for any business is to ensure that you are properly insured. There are many different types of insurance available for business owners. Knowing what types of coverage you will need are best determined by visiting with a professional insurance agent. When possible it is best to choose an agent who specializes in business insurance. In addition, prior to buying insurance discuss your business with your attorney. Explain what your business will be doing and how you might protect yourself from different contingencies.

Being a business owner requires that you take many risks. If you are not properly insured, some of the common risks that you will encounter may be just enough to end your business career. Please do not take this lightly. All of your policies should be reviewed on a yearly basis to make sure that you are covered for any and all types of losses. Some of the different types of insurance that you will definitely have to have from the beginning are listed here:

1. **Vehicle Insurance** - You must make sure you know exactly how much coverage that you have and talk to your agent; let him know what type of business you are in and who will be driving your vehicle. If you tell him that no one except you will be driving, but then allow your employees to drive, you have made a serious mistake. If

this person wrecks your vehicle, kills someone, or God knows what else could happen, you could be liable; best-case scenario is your insurance company would cover the loss, and then promptly drop your insurance. After something like this, you may have a hard time finding insurance coverage from another carrier. Don't think that it couldn't happen to you, because it could!

2. **Building Insurance** – If you are renting, I would suggest that you have renter's insurance. Talk to your agent for his advice on this. If you own your own building, you will need to have enough coverage to cover the cost of reconstructing your building. You would need to take into consideration inflation (cost of building will continually rise). So if you paid, for example $400,000 for your building three years ago, it may be worth a lot more today, depending on how good of a deal you got when you bought it. Again, make sure you're covered in case of disaster (you are in the business, so you know that it could happen!).

3. **Contents Coverage** – Your building insurance will not automatically cover the contents that are in your building. Some examples of contents would be your computers, your desks, file cabinets, and all equipment that you keep at your facility. This is definitely something you should make sure you have enough of!! This should be reviewed every year as you acquire more and more equipment and furniture for your growing business. Also ask about special coverage for the personal property of your customers that will be stored in your building during fire pack-outs.

4. **Inland Marine Insurance** – This is coverage for equipment that you have inside of your truck; for example, a truck-mount carpet cleaning machine, extractors, dehumidifiers, etc. The insurance on your vehicle alone would not cover the expense to your machine and/or other equipment if it were damaged or lost.

5. **Equipment Rider** – This is a policy that will cover specific equipment (usually anything that is valued at over $150). You would make up a list of your equipment that you want covered under the policy and give this to your insurance carrier (you would supply them with serial numbers to identify each specific piece of equipment). This insurance will cover each piece of equipment no matter where it is: on your truck, at your office, or in a client's home. Usually you will have a deductible, depending on the policy. There may be a deductible on each piece that you claim. Check with your insurance agent on this.

6. **Business Liability** - This is a large part of your insurance package as well. This is something you definitely MUST have. This will cover a broad range of perils that

could happen. Contact your insurance agent to get more information about what it does cover and what it does not. Also, your agent will be able to advise you on how much coverage you may need for this. One example would be if you were at a customer's home vacuuming their carpet and the cord on the vacuum damaged an expensive piece of crystal (let's say it is valued at $10,000). The customer will demand that you take care of this, and rightfully so. If you do not have insurance, you will have to pay out of pocket. Another thing to be aware of is the CCC clause (care, custody, and control); meaning that anything that is in your direct care, custody, or control is not going to be covered. In the case of the crystal breakage, it was covered because we were not actually cleaning the crystal; therefore, it was not in our control. If we were dusting the crystal and accidentally dropped it, it would not have been covered under a policy that excludes CCC.

7. **Business Interruption Rider** - This is something to consider. If your business is interrupted due to a disaster (your building burns down), this would help you out until you could get it running again. Please talk to an agent regarding the benefits and costs associated with this type of insurance. Most start-up companies do not purchase this because of all of the other start-up expenses that they have, but I think it is a good idea to at least check out the benefits.

8. **Workers Compensation Insurance** - This is mandatory in most states. If you are a sole proprietor and have no employees, then you may not be required to carry this insurance. Check with your agent to find out the requirements. If you are doing construction work and/or contract cleaning work, you will probably be required to have it. Our company does not subcontract to anyone that does not have workers comp. The reason being that if you hire, for example, a painter and he does not have worker's comp, you will have to cover him under your worker's comp policy. When you fill out your quarterly report, you would list him as if he was your employee and pay the rate for the type of work he did (i.e. painting and wallpaper, general carpentry). However, this we have found, is frowned on by your worker's comp provider (they would rather you hire people that have their own insurance). If you do decide to hire people without workers comp insurance, you should discuss with them in advance that you will be withholding an amount equal to what your insurance company will charge you to cover them under your policy.

9. **Health & life insurance** - You should not try to "save" by not purchasing a basic health insurance policy for yourself. Without you, the entrepreneur, the business

will not run. A lot of self-employed people will say that it is too expensive, but I can tell you from experience, it is not!! If you are healthy now, it will be easier to get, so don't delay in getting it. Just one major illness could put you out of business if you don't have adequate health insurance. There are different ways that you can lower your premiums—some are higher deductibles and higher co-pays. Shop around to get the best rates available. Nowadays it is very costly if you have an accident and do not have health insurance. An example follows: An emergency room visit with x-rays was billed to me at the amount of $2,800. I was there for one hour. Since I do have insurance, I only had to pay a $75 emergency co-pay. If you had to stay over-night, the charges would probably be in excess of $5,000. An extended stay would probably cost you your first-born! As far as your employees and health insurance, if you want good, long-term employees, offering some kind of health insurance to them may help and may draw people to your company if they know that they will be taken care of. Sometimes you may get lucky and hire someone that does not necessarily need the insurance (maybe they are covered by their spouse or their parents). Try to do a little investigating when you interview applicants to find out how important health insurance is to them. If you simply can't provide anything in the health insurance area and this is something that an individual is looking for as a benefit, you will be better off letting them look for employment elsewhere so they can find the benefits they need.

Marketing

Effectively finding and securing customers is the principal component of success for any type of business, across all sectors. From manufacturing, retail, to the service industry, we all need customers. Marketing and sales brings in the life blood of your business. Regardless of how great a concept or vision is, or how valuable a service can be to the end user, it will flop if there are no customers to make purchases. Great marketing is the manner in which your business transforms from a great idea with good employees and quality equipment to a profitable venture with a promising future. Good marketing finds the perfect candidates to become your customers and delivers them right to your front door.

There are countless niche groups that have the potential to refer business your way when marketing a cleaning and restoration business. The insurance industry is the primary niche that most restoration owners gravitate towards. However, they represent but one of many niche groups that can play a vital role in the growth of a restoration business. It makes perfect sense that the insurance industry is the primary target for most. After all if you have a mortgage, you have to have insurance. Therefore, agents and adjusters are perfectly positioned to be the link that you need to connect with the property owners that they insure, in their time of need. It stands to reason that those who have suffered some kind of damage or loss would be in the market for a restoration company. If you can get insurance companies to recommend your services to the consumer, you will have it made, right?

Well, yes, but it's not that easy. You will need to find ways to work through the competition and get your voice heard by those with influence inside the insurance industry. That in and of itself is a full-time job and a task that you might never master. The following sections will introduce you to the insurance industry as a whole, teach you some of the basics that you need to understand, and give you some proven strategies for getting the ear of those people who can make decisions.

THE RESTORATION INDUSTRY

The disaster restoration is a 70-80 billion dollar industry that serves the needs of federal, state, and municipal entities, commercial property owners, as well as residential owners, who have suffered from a disaster, be it man-made or natural type of disaster.

Restoration companies number in the thousands in the United States. The majority of restoration companies are independently owned and operated. The independents own the largest share of the market.

The market place can be further broken down by category of operator:

National firms

National firms are those who have the capability to respond to disasters anywhere around the country, with many offering worldwide service. These firms have very sophisticated logistics systems in place. They will usually have offices strategically located throughout the country to allow for rapid deployment of men and machinery when called upon. Not every national firm offers what you might view as full service; some will specialize in areas of disaster repair. You might have one national firm, for example, that specializes in large-scale drying only, while another does drying but also specializes in environmental issues such as fuel leaks, asbestos, weapons of mass destruction, etc. Yet you might have another national firm that does drying as well as rebuilding. The majority of these national firms are larger companies with highly sophisticated well-structured organizations. These firms will commonly employ structural engineers, biologists, architects, environmental experts as well as multiple levels of management all the way down to the field technicians.

These national firms can be further segmented by independently owned versus national franchise. Service Master, Servpro, and other franchise systems offer and tout national disaster response. The primary difference, as far as the actual response goes, is the way in which the disaster is handled. The national independent will employee his own workforce and equipment while the national franchise system will, through a well-planned and choreographed event, draw upon its many members. The franchise will typically have staging centers strategically located throughout the country and will allow for voluntary participation.

Similar to the franchise system of responding to national disaster is the affiliate, or network groups. These include Disaster Kleen-up International (DKI) with their 500 plus member base.

Likewise, their marketing efforts are also done on a nationwide scale, forging relationships and securing repair contracts well in advance of a disaster. The marketing and operations control centers of the national repair firms operate with military precision and are a lot like the experts at NOAA (National Oceanic and Atmospheric Administration), in that they study weather patterns and can predict with accuracy weather patterns that will be likely to cause major widespread damage. The obvious advantage is that they can begin deployment of materials and manpower in advance of the actual weather-related disaster. The firms that provide national coverage as their only forte pose little to no threat to the localized or even regional firms. The repair firms operate with military precision and are a lot like the experts at NOAA the national. The rest of the segmented group, when not on national assignment, does pose a competitive threat.

Regional Firms

Regional firms, as the name indicates, are those that provide large-scale disaster relief to a more regionalized geographical territory. Some may specialize in the Southwest region of the country while others may lay claim to the Midwest, or the Northeast, or the Southeast.

Like the nationals, these firms will vary in their capabilities and even in the types of services they offer. They share many of the other mentioned similarities with the nationals. Typically the regional, though well run and successful by anyone's standards, are not nearly as sophisticated or large as the nationals.

Storm Chasers

By definition, the storm chaser is one who specializes in working storms as they occur. This group can be further segmented into the following groups: The true professional well-equipped storm chaser and the amateur storm chaser.

The Professional Storm Chaser

These firms are often found at the scene of large-scale losses such as hurricanes or tornadoes. This group is capable of launching an army of men and materials to different areas of the country to respond to very large-scale disasters. Typically well funded and well equipped, they have the systems in place to move man and material from storm to storm with efficiency. Often times they are very capable of chasing a major storm two thousand miles away, while at the same time continuing to run their home base operation. They will typically choose their battles and not necessarily leap to the scene before having first assessed the potential returns against the potential pitfalls. It's not at all uncommon for a seasoned storm chaser to send an advanced team into an area of loss to gather pertinent information to assist in making the decision to stay or go. Nearly all of the country's largest storm chasing firms are independently owned and operated.

The Amateur Storm Chaser

The amateur storm chaser, on the contrary, is one who is typically a fraction of the size of the professional chaser, poorly funded, and far less organized. He is drawn by the allure of big money to areas of wide--scale destruction believing that he will find his pot of gold. Operating much like the lifestyle of a band of gypsy's, he will buy or rent a fleet of motor homes, buy every piece of drying equipment on credit from his local supplier, hock his children's educational fund, muster together his small army of workers, sometimes straight out of the drunk tank and head off to the promised land. Upon arrival, he learns in short order that the one thing that was most needed in this time of great opportunity, he doesn't possess. A plan. His restoration business back home that is just starting to flourish, now in its time of greatest need of guidance and nurturing, is left looking like an old western ghost town, withering away, or worse, being gobbled up by the shrewd competitor back home.

Go to any large-scale disaster around the country and you'll see first hand dozens, sometimes hundreds, of these well-meaning companies scrounging around looking for work. Ironically, it's this group that will often times not be paid for their services.

Localized Firm

A localized firm can be independently owned or part of a franchise system. They will typically have a well-defined geographical operating territory, whether self-imposed or as a condition of the franchise agreement.

Within his geographical area, he will offer his services. Each firm will choose his own area of specialty and will typically market the area based on his expertise.

Full Service Firm

Typically a full service firm will offer cleaning and restoration services to include emergency drying, smoke damage cleanup, carpet cleaning, and often times, rebuild services as well. This firm will generally either employ their own staff of tradespersons such as drywall, painters, etc., or will maintain a network of tradespersons who will be called in to assist with jobs on an as needed basis. Firms that subcontract the majority of their work are considered as general contractors or GC's. Some states and even communities require special licensing to become a GC. In our state of Missouri for example, there are no special requirements. Being a qualified GC doesn't necessarily mean that you would sub out all of your work. My own firm, for example, subs out our plumbing and electrical work, yet we maintain our own staff for many other disciplines such as drywall, painting, etc. On larger projects we sub out the drywall work to subcontractors who are better equipped to do the larger jobs.

As the GC you will assume many roles and responsibilities. You no longer have the luxury of the drying only firm in that you go in, do your job, and in a few days you are finished. The GC is responsible and fully expected to coordinate the entire process from day one through final walk through and completion.

General contracting has many advantages as well as disadvantages:

Advantages

Marketing – From a marketing standpoint being a general contractor is oftentimes looked upon favorably by the insurance community for which you will be marketing and hopefully getting referrals from. Many in the insurance community, especially adjusters, like the one-stop shopping advantage that comes from dealing with a qualified GC. An example of this might be a water damage loss. If the loss, for example, is a category three (grossly contaminated water) the carpet and pad will have to be removed and replaced. Perhaps the drywall must be sectioned up to four feet; the baseboards must be removed and replaced. Then a painter must be called in to paint after the drywall has been completed. And finally, the carpet that was removed early in the process must now be replaced.

Most adjusters just don't have the time or inclination to attempt to coordinate all the different trades required for this job. In fact, it's not even their duty to serve as a project manager. The adjuster saves a lot of time by not having to contact a water damage restorer, a painter, dry-waller, floor covering retailer, etc.

Disadvantages

Marketing - In regards to marketing your firm as a general contractor be cognizant that some adjusters wrongfully believe that the GC arrangement is going to mark up the services of each of his trades people in addition to adding profit and overhead onto the job, thus making the GC referral a much higher priced one. While it may be true in some cases that a GC is opportunistic with his pricing methods, across the board using the services of a GC is no more expensive than a specialist firm. Here is why: most GCs don't mark up their sub-trade's bills in an effort to realize more profit. Actually the profit, when using subcontractors, is on the front end of the arrangement. An example might be as follows; a full service firm acting as GC gets a fire damage claim.

The restoration GC will scope out the job site, sketch, and price it according to whichever pricing software program he utilizes. Next he will put the project or whatever portion of the project that his own firm isn't capable of performing, out on bid. It is a best practice to have two or three sub-trade firms look at the job site to determine if they have an interest in performing the required work. Once the sub tradesman has expressed an interest, the GC will indicate what the job is worth. In other words, we'll pay you X amount of money to do the job, usually 70-80% of the value of the job. The restoration company's bid for the drywall job utilizing Xactimate pricing = $5,678; The restoration GC offers the job to interested drywall sub-contractors at the 80% value of $4,542.50.

This arrangement can be mutually beneficial to both parties involved. If your market is facing a hefty volume of new construction starts, the selection of qualified contractors who might be willing to work for 80 cents on the dollar will be somewhat less. Likewise, if your local market economy is depressed, it will be much easier finding qualified subcontractors to accept this arrangement. There are material advantages to the subcontractor in that he does not need to spend as much on money on advertising, doesn't have to deal directly with the property owner, he gets paid much quicker by the restoration GC than he would if were working directly for the property owner. If all goes well he will have a regular source of work from your company. Most restoration GC's will establish a payment draw program to assist their trades people during the job. This is an added benefit on larger jobs where a subcontractor may need monies for his employees, materials, etc.

Specialized Firm

A specialized firm might be one that performs emergency mitigation and drying services but offers no repair services related to the loss. A mold remediation firm may specialize in mold related work, while subbing out the drying portion of the loss to a drying specialist.

Until recently, entrance into the restoration industry was relatively easy. Anyone with a carpet extractor and perhaps a fan or two could begin the process of marketing and building a restoration business. Fortunately for the professional restorer, changes during the past few years have made entrance into the industry much more difficult for the fly-by-nighter. The technological advancements, increased cost of equipment, and the necessity of training, especially in the water damage field, have for the first time positioned our industry as a professional one. <u>Our future looks bright!</u>

Today's professional restorer must possess a business acumen that allows him to fully understand the inner workings of this industry, but equally important he must understand how his business is intricately connected to so many others, including, but not limited to, the insurance industry.

As an industry trainer and business coach, I have had the good fortune of visiting with many restoration business owners. As you might imagine, I've spoken with some who are ultra successful, while others are struggling, even after having been in business for numerous years.

The one underlying common denominator that I've observed in each of the successful owners was their unwavering, almost religious-like dedication to adhering to a self-imposed code of ethics.

Many of the most successful operators small and large appear to be individuals that have thrown away the old game book. These are owners who are continually seeking better ways to improve upon the services they offer. They operate with an "outside the box" mentality. <u>There appears to be a strong correlation between operating outside of the box and long-term success.</u>

Major Trends Affecting the Restoration Industry

During the past several years there have been many technological advances in the restoration industry that directly affect the operations of all restoration companies. Many of these advances if not embraced and incorporated into the modern day operation have the potential to pose a palpable threat to their livelihood.

Restoration Networking Groups

In the past few years the restoration industry has seen an emergence of networking groups. These groups are touted as a way for the restoration owner to get more work, primarily through association. Each appear to offer something unique to the owner who joins, from access to the best training, with high tech tools to assist in a virtual claims process. Cost for membership will typically start at a minimum of $10,000 per year. This trend was spawned out of the need to battle insurance vendor programs. The philosophy is that if the networking group has a large enough membership base, they could then market to and potentially pick up some national insurance contracts for their membership base.

THE INSURANCE INDUSTRY OBSTACLES AND THREATS

Third Party Claims Administrators (TPA's)

During the past few years several third party claims administrators have emerged. These companies have begun building relationships with many of the insurers to handle much of their property damage claim work. They do bring a unique benefit for the participating restoration companies in that they are led by individuals who are well versed and have deep connections with the insurance industry. These claims management companies will each operate somewhat differently from the other. The purpose for the third party management companies is to save the insurer money by consolidating much of the workload associated with claims processing. Some will charge for the restoration owner's participation in the programs, while a handful tout that membership is free to qualified restoration owners. My own service company was involved for a short period of time with one of the newer third party claims companies and opted out of the program.

We did receive several jobs in a relatively short period of time from this company, so they are certainly a viable option for the restoration contractor who needs additional work. The drawback for our service company was in the way in which they took it upon themselves to manipulate our repair estimates.

Insurance Preferred Vendor Programs

One of the biggest hurdles facing the independent and many franchise restoration

contractors today is the dreaded insurance preferred vendor programs. Startup operators may be surprised to learn that many of the larger insurers utilize vendor programs
for the emergency mitigation as well as the repair portion of their insured's losses. With
these programs many independents are unfairly shut out of the mitigation work as well
as being locked out of the lucrative repair portion of the job.

We will explore the insurance vendor programs in detail in this book. It is important to note that these programs have been around for a very long time, and contrary to
what many may believe, I don't see these programs withering away anytime soon. The
top tier insurance rascals will place another obstacle in front of the insured's, as well as
the restoration contractors. They specialize in the cat and mouse game. What the reader should know is that there are countless restoration owners who are long retired and
very wealthy as a result of working in the insurance repair industry through the vendor
programs. It is equally important to note and to understand that a high quality restoration operator can survive and thrive even if he chooses not to participate in insurance
vendor programs. The wealth that you generate from the cleaning and restoration field
will be commensurate with the work and dedication that you give.

Many restorers of every size and shape have no interest in participating in insurance
vendor programs. I know many who were listed in vendor programs only to have opted
out after a short period of time. These restorers typically site difficult working relationships with the vendor managers, in addition to the many restrictions imposed on the
restorer by the Insurer, as the primary reason for opting out of the program.

I'll share an example of just how frustrating insurance vendor programs can be for
all parties involved. A couple of years back one of my neighbors suffered a large water
loss. She lives about five homes down from mine. Her neighbor just happens to work
at the one of the local franchises and of course always parks his brightly colored truck
directly in front of her home.

I returned home the evening of the loss to see several trucks belonging to a local
franchise parked in front of her home. They did their normal daily monitoring which
went on for a few days. By the third day, one of the local independents arrives and his
crews begin demolition work on the lady's home. They were at the job site on and off
for the next few weeks.

A couple of months later the owner of the independent company happened to stop by my office for a visit. I finally had the opportunity to hear the whole story. As it turns out, according to him, the little old lady filed a claim with her insurance company. They immediately told her that they would call franchise #1 to initiate the recovery process. She informed the insurer that she did not want this gentleman, who also happened to be her neighbor coming into to her home for personal reasons. The insurer then calls company #2 who is listed on their vendor program to get started with the mitigation work. By this time the independent has been notified about coming out to the site for the repair portion of the job. The snag with this arrangement was that neither the independent or franchise were informed of this decision by the claims adjuster. This national insurer has a propensity to randomly split their claims, with one company being assigned the mitigation and drying services, while the other vendor is assigned the repair portion of the job. So here it was, according to the independent, a fight for control of the job. They must have looked like two taxicabs drivers at LaGuardia, fighting over international arrivals for a fare. This is just an unfair way in which to operate. Here the franchise had done a great job in drying and should have been entitled to do the repair work. On the other hand the independent does great repair work and after all, he is also on the vendor program, so he felt that he was entitled to take the work. He was angry because he wasn't called in for the drying portion of the job, which of course is the more lucrative of the two. At the end of the day it was the elderly lady who got screwed! Luckily for me I just happen to live down the street and had a front row seat to enjoy the show.

The preferred vendor application and its process with the detailed request and requirements would probably surprise many tender feet. They are more restrictive than one might imagine.

The following are a sampling of the questions that one can expect to see on most of the national insurers vendor program pre-qualification forms. Note that the typical pre-qualification form is divided into these basic sections:

Operational Information

• Type of business – corporation, sole proprietor, partnership, etc.
• Business address – location.
• State employer ID#
• License number. (This number is referring to contractors license).
• Is your company listed in the phone book? White pages, yellow pages? What

category heading?

- Principal types of work - Water damage, smoke cleanup, general construction, etc.
- Preferred job size – Small up $3,500, medium $10,000-$20,000, extra large in excess of $100,000.
- Service ability – What is your service coverage area by zip code. Do you have an answering service? If yes, telephone number.
- Names of officers, partners or owner, with names and titles.
- Names of key personnel and their positions.
- Names of employees and their positions. Full or part time.
- Principal type of work performed with own work force.
- Do you and your sub-contractors operate under a standard form of union agreement? Yes or no.
- List typical contracts completed last four years or less. Year, name, and location of jobs and the size of job in dollars.
- What is the total square footage of your facility? Is your facility leased or owned.
- Number of years in business.
- Are your field personnel required to wear uniforms? Yes or no.
- Are your estimators paid by salary, or salary plus commission? If commission is paid, on what do they base the commission?
- Company's annual work volume, in dollars. Last four years starting with most current.
- States in which you are licensed.
- Have you ever at any time failed to complete a contract. Yes or no. If yes, submit details on a separate sheet.
- Are there any judgments, claims, or suits pending or outstanding against you? Yes or no. If yes, submit details on separate sheet.
- Has your license ever been revoked or suspended? Yes or no. If yes, submit details on separate sheet.
- Do you warranty your work force and sub-contractors workmanship? Yes or no. If yes what is the warranty period.
- Have you performed insurance restoration for this insurance company? If yes, insured's name, claim number, location and amount of the job.
- Do you or members of your company belong to any professional organizations? Yes or no. If yes, list names and organizations on separate sheet.

System Information Section

- Does your office use a personal computer? Yes or no. If yes, what brand, size and operating system.
- Do you use a digital camera for job/photo documentation? Yes or no. If yes, what brand and model.
- Does your office have a copy machine? Yes or no.
- Do you use automation to bid/estimate jobs? Yes or no. If yes, name of application(s).
- Do you use a pager? Yes or no. If yes, what brand and model, pager number.
- Does your office have a fax machine? Yes or no. Fax number.

References: Provide three references from the following (material supplier and sub-contractor). Material supplier name, contact person and phone number. Subcontractor name, contact person and phone number.

Work In Progress Under Contract: Percentage completed, name and location of jobs and phone number. Total work in progress under contract.

Bank(s): Where company maintains accounts.

Contractor Insurance: Name of insuring companies, general liability limits, workers compensation limits.

Bonding: Bonding capacity, bonding company.

Authorization: Do you authorize Insurer to make inquiries into your credit, tour your facility, and inspect the business operation. Yes or no.

Financial Statement: Current assets, fixed assets (depreciated) other assets, total assets.

Current Liabilities: Long-term liabilities, total liabilities.

Net Worth:

Date of last Balance Sheet: ___/___/ **prepared by:** _____

Overcoming the Vendor Program

If you are opposed to joining a franchise that has established vendor agreements in place with the larger insurers, you will need to develop innovative strategies that allow you to get your share of the insurance restoration pie. If you employ creatively a strong marketing and sales approach that is relevant, and good old-fashioned tenacity, you will rise to the top!

One such approach when attempting to gain referrals directly from claims adjusters, claims offices and even agents is to offer your service for the areas where the insurer lacks coverage. All too often a well-meaning restorer goes out and markets to adjusters looking for referrals. Obviously, when first meeting this adjuster, he is going to inform you that their company has a preferred vendor program and already has restoration companies that are listed. When you hear this, don't get discouraged and leave with your tail between your legs. This adjuster is only telling you the truth. The company does have a vendors' program. It would do him little good to get you all excited by telling you he would start referring your firm when in fact it is his job to use the vendors on the list. Here is what you need to know, especially if you are new to marketing restoration services. In much of the country there are overlapping geographical areas that are not serviced by these preferred vendors. Even with all the franchises combined they couldn't possibly cover every square mile. This is your area friend, stake claim to it right away.

I recall meeting with a senior claims adjuster a long time ago who told me that there was absolutely nothing he could do for me in regards to referring my company. He informed me that his company had a directive to refer only those who were approved on their preferred vendor program. As I was getting ready to walk away with my head held low, feeling like a whipped pup and all discouraged, he said: "That is, not unless you are willing to do work in "X" location."

I began to listen intently as he voiced that he would be happy to work with me in those areas where the vendors were unwilling to go.

Just then I recalled a quote from who I believed was the late Sam Walton founder of Wal-Mart. I believe it was Sam who had been asked about his success in building the Wal-Mart Empire. His reply was something to effect of "We go to where they ain't". What a brilliant strategy "to go where they ain't." While the K-Marts, Sears and other behemoths sat around getting fat and taking their customers for granted, old Sam was taking the game to them. Here he was setting up these stores in small towns across the country and at the same time winning loyalty from those who had been forced to suffer under the rule of K-Mart and others for so long. Eventually, Sam circled his wagons around their stronghold and literally choked the life out of them.

This is one of the strategies I was alluding to when I stated that you will have to get creative and employ some innovative strategies. There are many vendors who make enough money working right in their own back yard and have no desire to service insurance jobs outside of their area. Ask the claims adjuster, claims managers, agents and others involved in the process to give your company a shot at serving their customers who are in these fringe areas.

As if the dreaded vendor program wasn't a big enough blow to the independent restorers, the insurance industry continues to look for efficient ways in which to squeeze the insured's. There has been a trend in raising the deductible on the standard homeowner policy. With the average water loss coming in at around $3,000 and with the deductibles beginning to climb to around $2,000 the policy holder may give second thought to filing a claim as the deductible is going to cover the largest part of the claim. And if they do have the work performed by a professional restorer the entire attitude typically changes from one of the insured not being concerned with cost as the insurance company is paying for it, to one of now we've got to scrutinize every minute detail of this job. We'll get into much more detail when we discuss marketing to the agents and adjusters.

The competitive nature of the industry is tough.

Make no mistake about it! The cleaning and restoration industry is very competitive. I've had the opportunity to witness firsthand what happens when your guard has been let down. Personally, I've always felt like the industry was big enough for everyone involved. However, there are those with the mentality that they want it all, with an insatiable appetite for greed, control, and power. They have an unsavory penchant for money and will get it at any cost, even if it means treading on a competitor. I'm reminded of an Arabian Proverb; *Trust in Allah, but tie your camel close.*

They will attempt to discredit your service whenever they can, and will even go as far as to sabotage your company. Staying one step ahead of these slippery fish at times feels like a game of cat and mouse.

I'll share a story that perfectly describes the competitive nature of the industry. We were called in to look at a fire damage loss. This loss was extensive in size and damage; a six-unit apartment building had caught fire on a cold Christmas Eve. At the time we were besieged with work and not particularly interested in taking on another project, especially on this scale. My arrival was timed to meet with the senior claims adjuster that had made the call to me about the fire. Subsequent to the usual pleasantries we began the damage assessment process. I finalized my initial estimate within two days of the initial scope. The estimated cost to repair this structure was $450,000. Of course by now my opinion had changed and was in fact excited with the prospect of getting this job. I met with the owner and adjuster the following day. The owner, a very intelligent and successful woman, asked me a few questions. One of her questions was regarding a competitor who has also submitted an estimate for the repair of the six-plex. Up until this point I was oblivious to the news that a competitor had even bid on this job. The specific question that she had asked me was; what was my opinion of the owner of the competing business? I thought about it for a moment and replied, that I thought he was a nice enough guy, and I believed that yes, his company would be capable of restoring her property. I even went so far as to say that I didn't believe she would find any fault with his work. I wasn't lying to the woman, that's exactly what my thoughts were regarding him and his business.

Now here's the kicker! She looked me square in the eyes and said; Ivan I'd like to go with your company. Can you get started right away? After saying yes, she went on to explain to me why she chose my firm and not our competitor. The competitor wanted the job so bad that when she had informed him that she had also received an estimate from my company, he thought as a last ditch effort, he would attempt to discredit my company. He asked the owner why she would choose Aerodry as they are just a carpet cleaning company; they know nothing about fire restoration. She told me some time later that she didn't choose us because of the way he bad mouthed us, but chose us, because of the way I didn't bad mouth them.

Moral of the story—never say anything bad about your competitors even when they have nothing nice to say about you!

Understanding how the insurance industry works.

In 1993 the Midwest had suffered major flooding. In fact it was the worst widespread flood in 500 years. The Missouri and Mississippi along with several other large rivers in our state had left their banks and caused massive damage throughout the state of Missouri. At the time we were a smaller drying company that really didn't have the equipment, manpower or knowledge to address the larger commercial drying opportunities that were everywhere you looked.

In the early stages of the flooding I received a call from the owner of one of the larger national storm chasing companies informing me that he and his advanced team would be visiting our city, in an effort to drum up some large drying jobs. He asked if I would have an interest in helping him locate larger commercial buildings that had been damaged, or would likely be damaged by the flood. In return he said he would give me a nice percentage on the proceeds if he landed any drying jobs that I took him to visit. We visited several commercial properties including a landmark hotel in my community that had been flooded.

While we were visiting this landmark hotel I watched him carefully in an effort to see what differences there were between him, the highly experienced restorer and me, the relatively inexperienced restorer. As you might imagine, the differences were stark. As we arrived at the property, there were adjusters, the hotel owners and their property managers viewing the damages. As he approached these individuals he began to speak in a vernacular that was totally foreign to me. Not once did he mention his mega fleet of large capacity dryers to this group. He went right to the business of carrying on in this language that these people seemed to recognize.

As I later learned the language that he was speaking is common amongst those who work in the insurance industry, as well as those who manage large commercial properties. He sounded more like an insurance man or someone with a risk management background. Later that evening we spent quite a bit of time just talking and he generously answered my many questions. I specifically asked him why it was that he spoke that language to those guys and why it was that he never mentioned anything at all about his impressive arsenal of drying equipment.

He explained to me that he was speaking this strange language because it was the language that they would best relate to. He told me that one of the best things a restorer can do marketing wise is to study the language of those who you plan on marketing to. "Insurance guys, he said, relate better to those who understand their world and are much more likely to choose working with someone who understands exactly how the game is played before the game actually starts."

He said, "Adjusters, especially those working larger type of losses, don't have the time or interest to be training a new guy on how the game is played." He used words like re-insurance, co-insurance, lost revenues, environmental concerns, etc., because they understand those words.

Then he went on to say that desiccant dryers, air movers, and extractors mean absolutely nothing to them. I would strongly encourage any reader that is unfamiliar with how the insurance industry works, including the commonly used terminology, to pay special attention to the following section.

How the Insurance Industry Works

The insurance restoration industry is a 60-80 billion dollar industry. Americans spend billions of dollars every year on premiums and the insurance companies spend billions in paying out on losses, be it auto, liability, workmen's' comp, health or property.

Insurance is a pooled risk. The companies look at your home in several ways, such as size, location, age and other criteria. The underwriters know that a certain percentage of homes will catch fire or flood. Based on how the house is constructed it will cost X number of dollars. With the law of averages a customer is assigned a dollar amount in premium. The customer will choose which company they will go with for all sorts of reasons. Some will base opinion on price, some on name recognition and some on claims paying experience.

The agent has the first contact with the customer. It is their job to place the right amount of coverage on a person's property. After the customer agrees on the coverage amount they will pay their premiums.

The insurance company collects all the premiums and then invests it how they see fit. Then when a person has a covered loss they will put the estimated amount of damages in reserve; this is how the company "pools" the risk. They lump everyone's premium into an investment account. The company makes more on the investments than on the premium. When you have a claim and it's a covered peril they pay. The homeowner then has a right to use any repair firm they choose to fix their house.

How Does a Claim Work – Start to Finish

When a person has a loss, they usually report it. The insured will call their agent first; they are the only ones the insured knows. After the agent hangs up they will call the claim department and/or a restoration company. The insurer assigns a claim number to the loss and will dispatch an adjuster out to the loss to see it if is indeed a "covered" loss. There are covered and non-covered losses, which is the adjuster's job to determine and to also determine the financial level of responsibility on the part of the insurer. If it is a covered loss then the homeowner or adjuster will call a reputable restoration company to mitigate the loss and rebuild if necessary. We do what it takes to restore the homeowner's home to pre-loss condition and then the adjuster cuts a check to the insured.

INSURANCE TERMS

Actual Cash Value:

This term is commonly abbreviated ACV. Most frequently this represents the re-placement cost minus depreciation. In some cases, other factors may be considered in establishing the ACV. When replacement cost coverage is provided, most policies pay the actual cash value until the claimant proves that he has actually replaced the item, at which time the company pays the difference.

All Risk:

A policy that covers all perils except those specifically excluded appraisal clause:

Homeowner's policies and many others specify that if the parties fail to agree on the amount of a loss, either party may request arbitration. The procedure is called "going to appraisal", the details of which are spelled out in the policy.

Bailey:

Legal responsibility is assumed when one party takes the property of another into its care and custody. Property belonging to others is covered by Bailey insurance. The party who has accepted custody of another's property is called a Baylor.

Coinsurance:

When more than one insurance company has coverage on a property, a covered loss is divided according to the proportion of coverage each company has, relative to the total. If inadequate coverage has been purchased, the property owner is regarded as the co-insurer, and pays his "portion" of the loss.

Coinsurance Requirement:

A policy may require that the policyholder carry insurance for a stated percentage of the property's replacement cost. If the amount of insurance carried does not meet the requirement, the insurer is obligated to pay only the portion of the loss, which corresponds with their share of the coverage.

Consequential Loss:

This is a loss that occurs as a secondary result of a direct loss. For example, if a claimant missed work or lost their job because of a fire, their lost income is considered a consequential loss, not a direct loss under their fire policy.

Coverage:

Coverage relates to the specific perils and property to which an insurance policy responds. To say that a particular peril, loss, or type of property is not covered means that it is not insured by that policy.

Deductible:

An amount automatically deducted from any claim. The claimant is presumed to pay this initial amount in exchange for a lower premium. Large organizations may have extremely high deductibles, making them self-insured for any loss under that amount.

Depreciation:

An amount deducted from the replacement cost to compensate for loss in value due to age, wear, obsolescence, or other factor.

Direct Loss:

Insurance coverage responds to losses directly caused by a covered peril.

Draft Authority:

Some insurance agents, designated special agents, and licensed staff may be granted permission by an insurance company to settle and pay losses up to some dollar limit. This is the amount of the agent or adjuster's draft authority. They must obtain permission from the insurance company before approving payments that exceed their authority.

Endorsement:

A change in the policy conditions; usually shown as a reference number that corresponds to a standardized form. For example, an actual cash value policy may be changed to replacement cost by the addition of a replacement cost endorsement.

First Party Loss:

An insurance loss where the claimant is a named payee on the policy.

Hostile Fire:

A fire that escapes a normal and intended location for a fire. For example, a fire in a chimney flue is hostile, whereas one confined to a fireplace is "friendly". Insurance coverage responds to hostile fire damage.

Improvements & Betterments:

Changes made by a tenant on property owned by others. The tenant may be insured for the improvements and betterments he provides. Improvements and betterments provided by former tenants usually are considered to belong to the building owner.

Insurable Interest:

In order to obtain insurance, the policyholder must have an "insurable interest" in the property insured. This need not be outright ownership. A leasehold interest or other economic right may be considered an insurable interest. The significant idea is that an uninvolved outside party may not insure someone else's property.

Insured:

The party of parties indemnified by the policy sometimes called the "Named Insured". Only parties named on the policy are covered.

Like Kind and Quality:

The standard by which replacement cost is evaluated. It is not necessary to provide an identical replacement.

Loss of Rents:

An amount payable under loss of rents coverage to compensate a property owner for lost rental income as a result of damage. Usually the rental period is fixed at a reasonable time for repairs to the performed.

Loss of Use:

Formerly this coverage was called additional living expense, or ALE. This is the additional amount that an insured has paid in order to maintain his normal lifestyle when a covered loss prevents use of their dwelling. The insured's normal living expenses are deducted when calculating this amount.

Loss Report:

When an agency is notified that a loss has occurred to one of its policyholders, it immediately files a loss report with the insurance company, which spells out the loss and policy details. This is also called an "Accord form".

Mortgage Clause:

In building policies it is common to protect the lender with a mortgagee clause, which stipulates that the mortgagee will be named as payee on any check or draft issued under the policy. Where both dwelling and contents coverage's are involved, it is usual for the real estate mortgagee to be named only on the building check, since it has no rights to the personal property.

Named Peril:

A policy in which only certain designated perils are covered. Any perils not named are excluded.

Non-Waiver Agreement:

When an insurance company actively investigates a loss, there is an implication that it has agreed to cover the loss. If the company wishes to investigate without waiving its right to deny the claim, it obtains a non-waiver agreement from the insured, in which the insured agrees that the insurance company does not waive its rights by investigating the loss.

Notification:

Policies have certain notification requirements for the policyholder. This includes notification of the company of the loss as quickly as possible. Failure to promptly notify the company may result in loss of coverage if the company's rights are found to have been jeopardized.

Payee:

A party named on the policy, whose name the insurance company is obligated to include on any check or draft issued on a claim. Payees in addition to the insured may be a mortgage company, landlord, leasing agency, or other party with a direct financial interest in the property.

Peril:

A specific type of damage. For example: fire, smoke, water, vandalism, and malicious mischief.

Policy Limits:

The upper dollar limit shown on the policy, or the maximum amount that can be paid. Different coverages usually carry different limits in the same policy.

Power of Attorney:

A document giving another party the right to act as an agent in their behalf for some specific purpose for a stated period of time.

Proof of Loss:

A legal notification sent to the insurance company by a claimant, which shows the date of loss, kind of loss, the identity of the insured, and the amount of the claim under each coverage. This is the formal claim submitted to the carrier.

Release:

A form which, when signed, waives all future claims for that loss by the insured or other claimant.

Replacement Cost:

Sometimes called replacement cost new. Replacement cost is the cost of obtaining a new item of the same kind and quality as a damaged property. Some limitations accompany this coverage, relating to artworks, antiques, and unserviceable items. Individual items are covered to a maximum of 400% of actual cash value at the time of the loss.

Reserve:

State insurance codes require that insurance companies set aside funds to cover each loss immediately after they receive notification of the loss. One function of the adjuster is to establish the proper reserve amount after inspecting the loss site.

Scheduled Property:

Scheduled property is individually listed on the policy, accompanied by a specific value. Scheduled property is covered under a different type of policy, usually a personal property floater.

Subrogation:

Policies require that the policyholder give the insurance company the right to act in his behalf against another party. For example, if the insurance company believes that a loss was caused by the negligence of a third party, it may bring suit on behalf of the insured in order to regain any monies they have paid on that claim. This conveying of rights to the company is known as subrogation.

Third Party Loss:

A liability claim where someone not party to the insurance agreement makes a claim against an insured, which submits the claim to his liability carrier.

Time Limits:

States impose requirements on insurance companies specifying how soon the insurer must act in response to a proof of loss submitted by a policyholder. Sixty days is a common limit.

Unscheduled Personal Property:

Personal property insured under the contents property section of homeowner's policies. A lump sum, usually a percentage of the building coverage, is shown as the dollar limit for personal property. The individual items of a personal property are not listed.

The Sheet:

This is a term that is often used to describe the estimate or cost of damages. Many adjusters and claims managers refer to our estimates as sheets.

Research

Surprisingly enough, most of the research you must gather on the agent is very simple to get. You can simply ask the agent. Most people love to talk about themselves. This is referred to as the needs analysis. The few minutes you spend on researching before you enter an office on a cold call will make all the difference in the world. We break our own research into two categories: business research, and personal research. Much of the research can be done prior to your first visit. Once you begin your regular scheduled visits you will pick up a substantial amount of information.

Once you gather your research put it to use. If you know that a certain agent is into hunting, then you should subscribe to a hunting magazine, or perhaps you could join or support the local hunting club. When you run across any information that is hunting related, pass it onto the agent. Sure the agent may already have the knowledge; however it shows that you have his personal interest in mind. More important is that it gives you something to talk about during your visits. I would strongly suggest that issues relating to politics and religion be avoided.

Each time that you are marketing to a different community you must spend a few minutes gathering research information on that community. We maintain a file folder on each community that we market to. This information will be beneficial when visiting the agents of those communities.

There are several areas of the typical community to gather your information. The very first and most important visit should be to the Chamber of Commerce. An early morning visit to the local café will yield a ton of information on the community. Ask the waitress questions about the town like:

• Populations and other demographics information?
• Number of housing units?
• History of the community?

Business Research

• How old is the agency?
• Is the agent a first, second, third generation agent?
• Is the agent an independent or company agent?
• How many agents are there in the company?
• Has the agent received awards or recognition from the company?
• Does the agent sell financial vehicles; stocks, mutual funds etc., as well as insurance?
• Size of the agent's book of business?
• Number of losses per year?
• How the agent handles his losses?
• How long has the agent been at this physical location?
• Social demographics of the community or suburb in which he works?

Personal Research

• Agent's hobbies?
• Co-decision maker's hobbies?
• Birthday of agents and key co-decision maker?
• Educational background?
• Why the agent chose his profession?
• Spousal information?
• Children?

- Prior work history?
- Community involvement?

As business owners we have all met other owners who appear to always have everything happen just right for the business. Lucky stiffs. It seems like nearly everything that they touch turns to gold. We have also met those who appear to work their butts off only to end up with the short end of the stick.

During my many contacts with insurance adjusters I've learned that by and large, most claims adjusters want the same basic things from their restoration contractors. Below I've compiled a list, in no particular order, of the top wants and needs from most adjusters. For the reader I would encourage you to ask adjusters that you work with and market to, what it is that they would really like to see in a restoration company. Then build your company to fulfill those needs. You'll never know unless you ask!

Adjusters "Hot Buttons"

- Well written, timely estimates
- Knowledgeable estimators honesty and integrity
- Restoration company to be a clear communicator
- Quality work

Well Written Estimates

For those who don't have a lot of experience in writing estimates, or if you have slipped into the habit of writing sloppy estimates, and don't put much more than the basics into your estimates, then you are missing out on an excellent growth building opportunity. Of all the things a cleaning and restoration owner can do to get new business and to guarantee that the existing referrals continue to flow in, writing excellent estimates is within the top three.

Many find the tasks of writing estimates boring, complicated, and confusing. Actually, I'd agree that they can be time consuming, and yes at times they can become complicated, however, like every other aspect of the business the more you practice the better you get.

A very important factor often overlooked by those writing estimates is that it's not only the claims adjuster who reads the estimate. Most insurers' process estimates through an established chain of command. After the field adjuster has reviewed your estimate it will often times be forwarded to his claims manager for review. For the poorly written estimate, this is where the scrutinizing begins. And once the scrutinizing begins, the price-chopping axe is sure to follow.

In our administrative manual we discuss how important it is to always maintain leverage in your business when it comes to collecting payment for the work your company performs. For this aspect of the business we maintain this leverage through our written, legally binding contracts. When it comes to insurance restoration and repair, your scope and estimate are your leverage. This statement applies to drying services as well as full service firms.

There are several estimating programs available to the professional restorer. We use Exactimate, but the type that you use isn't nearly as important as the content that you insert into your estimate. Even a well thought out hand-written estimate is better than a poorly written estimate using one of the more popular estimating programs.

Writing an Award Winning Estimate

Once you have your estimating systems in place, you must take this and market it to all of your agent and adjuster contacts. We have found that a face-to-face meeting with adjusters works best for sharing a well-written estimate and discussing your scoping capabilities.

If you find yourself weak in the area of understanding the typical building components of residential and commercial construction, then it might be a good idea to bring someone into the company who is strong in that field. As we discussed in an earlier section, sometimes the interest of a growing business is best served by recruiting an individual with experience that can be applied towards your own operation. Writing scopes and estimates is all part of being involved in the cleaning and restoration industry.

A funny thing happens when a well-written estimate is compared next to a poorly written estimate. People automatically assume that the better-written estimate comes from a better-run company. Obviously this isn't always the truth, and I'm not implying that a poorly written estimate means that the company is poorly run. However, first impressions are lasting impressions. Your estimate is the first impression the reader gets regarding the internal workings of your company. Sure they have met your people and found them to be nice, clean-cut individuals. But your estimate is a reflection of your management style. Once again this is another perfect opportunity to build your brand.

This isn't to say that if you are inexperienced that you cannot learn to scope and estimate. When I first started scoping and estimating I had absolutely no experience whatsoever. I didn't know the difference between drywall and baseboards. My experience came through learning by trial and error. As we began to take on more fire damage jobs, I invested in the Exactware Construction Training program. This self-paced learning program was the single best investment I had made regarding learning the typical parts that make up a structure. Today we employee project managers who also serve as estimators. If I were to do it all over again, I would have brought a project manager/estimator to the team from day one. We lost out on many decent-sized jobs in the early days due largely to my lack of knowledge of scoping and estimating.

Well-written estimates will emphasize the importance you place on details. It's this ability to draft well-written estimates that will serve to differentiate your company form the rest of the pack.

A well-written estimate begins with an understanding of the emotional stress that the insured is under during their time of loss. Be thoughtful of your client. Think about how you would want the situation handled if you were the one suffering from the loss.

Submit Timely Estimates

An estimate submitted within a reasonable period of time is another one of the top three wants of the typical adjuster. Even if you're dealing with a company adjuster who has written his own estimate, he still needs to see your estimate to come to a final conclusion on the total estimated repair cost. For some of the smaller mutual insurers time becomes important as they must have an estimate to help in establishing reserves which are required by law to be set aside to cover the loss.

We structure our estimates to fit the particular service we are providing. An example might be: The mitigation estimate, the personal property estimate, the initial structural repair estimate and the final structural repair estimate.

I think it is important to mention that many restorers wait way too long to submit their estimates. It's understandable that some repair jobs are more complex and will require the restorer to gather estimates from various trades' people, however, taking two to three weeks to submit at least an initial estimate is too long.

For our service company we market that our initial structural repair estimates will be submitted within three working days of our on-site visit. For our mitigation work we submit our estimate upon completion of the mitigation work, or sooner.

In our company we have a project manager/estimator that focuses on scoping and writing estimates. Prior to having a PM, our estimates sometimes took an excessive amount of time to complete.

I took the opportunity to ask several adjusters what their thoughts were regarding restoration contractors, my own company included, on taking an excessive amount of time to draft an estimate. Almost unanimously, they said that they thought the primary reason was that either the contractor was a mom and pop type that just didn't have the knowhow or skill to properly write an estimate, or that the restorer lacked organizational skills to manage multiple jobs. Each adjuster who was asked this question had the mindset that a poorly written and/or slowly produced estimate was an indicator that the restorer was probably up to his neck in work and was probably a company that lacked organizational skills.

Like everything else that your company offers, if you don't take advantage of your estimating skills by marketing it, then you are wasting an opportunity. When we first started offering and marketing set time lines for completed estimates to agents and adjusters we did so using an honest performance scoring system. In other words, if we were two days behind the three day promise we would mention this to the agent and adjuster when we submit the estimate, and would also indicate that we are working terribly hard to live up to our promise of three days.

I never made excuses for our estimate tardiness. We just informed them of our actual estimate submitted time and kept improving on those times. Finally we reached a position of having 95% of all our estimates delivered as promised within the promised time. We certainly brag about this 95% success rate any chance we get. What I had learned was that by building up and keeping score of our estimate turnaround time, I had inadvertently made this self-imposed time line an advantage to our company. Not necessarily because of the self-imposed three day turnaround time, but because we actually made the issue important to our company which in turn benefited the adjusters. We post the estimate turnaround time on each of the estimates that our company submits.

Every time an adjuster or the claims manager receives our estimate they cannot help but to take note of the time. We also use this opportunity to reinforce our success rate. Think about this. Let's assume that you were to adopt a similar program to ours in terms of guaranteed estimate submission times. Now assume that you have been marketing to an insurer that has referred you a couple of times but for the most part overlooks your firm for one of your competitors.

You have marketed your turnaround times to every agent, adjuster and claims manager within this particular company. Even if they are currently not referring you the next time they run into a situation with a competitor where they basically have to pull teeth to get the estimate submitted who do you think they will be thinking of? Of course, the company that has taken the bold steps of building a system to allow them to expedite estimate turnaround times.

Note: Obviously this type of program only works if you are committed to making it work. To make this type of program work will require a major commitment from management in allocating whatever resources may be necessary to make it work. I know of many restorers who accomplish consistent turnaround times by employing laptops for in-the-field use.

Ask any adjuster about the importance of working with qualified restoration estimators and they'll likely tell you that the estimator's qualifications are of great importance. When you think about it, a restoration estimator is perfectly positioned to offer expert help to both the insured and the insurer, should he chose to take the impartial road to performing restoration work.

Here is the important article to remember: **As a restorer you are working for the insured—not the insurer!** The insurance company may be the one cutting the check for the repair, but it is the insured that you are obligated to first and foremost. Even so, padding estimates in the favor of the insured or for your own financial gain is one sure way to get black listed by the insurance community and for good reason, too! This behavior is not only morally wrong, it borders on being illegal.

- An estimator, be they employed by a restoration contractor or by an insurer, are brought into a property loss to determine the costs associated with repairing the property to pre-loss conditions. The only way that this can be done with accuracy is if the estimator is impartial and doesn't let his emotions weigh in on his decision making process. His expertise and experience allows them to offer professional opinions on a wide variety of damage related situations.
- The estimator is placed into a unique position that has the potential to upset the insured or the adjuster assigned to the claim. It is important that the estimator fully understand the difference between fact and opinion; between what is known as opposed

to what is suspected, or assumed. And equally important is the manner in which the estimator communicates these facts.

Webster defines fact as follows: Something that actually occurred or exists. Something that has real and demonstrable existence. When you as the estimator are performing your services, whether it is speaking with the claimant or in writing the estimate, keep in mind that unless what you are writing or speaking about was directly observed by you is not a fact. Fact can only be a statement describing an event or circumstance of which you had directly observed, or which is verifiable by evidence.

Below is an example of how not separating fact from guessing can lead into trouble for the restorer:

Fact – the intense heat associated with this kitchen fire necessitates complete removal and replacement of cabinetry. Besides non removable soot, the upper cabinets have sustained moderate to heavy charring.

Non-Fact – All of the electrical wire in this unit must be replaced due to the heavy soot deposits on the walls.

(Note - that no supporting evidence is attached to this statement). This is not fact. It's not an opinion either - It's a statement that might be made by an overzealous contractor.

Opinion – The heavy soot deposit coupled with the moderate to heavy char on the cabinets indicate that further demolition must be performed, to allow for a more in-depth scope prior to finalizing an "Accurate Scope and Repair Estimate."

Insured's Needs

Addressing the needs of the insured is one of the areas that most estimators find difficulty in dealing with. Ask any seasoned estimator about the insured's needs versus their desires and you will likely learn that most will agree that needs and desires seem to get clouded for the insured on the typical loss, especially if the loss is an insurance covered loss. Your estimate must be based solely on facts and guided by your experience. Understanding that their needs may not necessarily be the same as their desires is fundamental to getting off to a great start.

An example might be when a claimant indicates that the cabinetry in their kitchen needs to be replaced after an occurrence of light smoke damage. While this may be indeed be their belief it may also be their desire. You, as the trained estimator, must make the call. It will require that you possess the ability to articulate your opinion in such a manner as to not give off the impression that you are underestimating or under-scoring the loss.

Marketing to Claims Managers

Marketing to claims managers and to the staff that work at the claims office is an important strategy that will be an overall part of a restoration marketing campaign. Before attempting to market to the claims offices there are a couple of important thing that you must be aware of and prepare for in advance of calling on the claims managers. The most important thing to remember is that prior to ever stepping foot in a claims manager's office, you have visited or at least contacted several of the field adjusters first. A claims manager has a lot of influence and can spread your name rapidly to each of his field adjusters. However, to just drop in to a claims office expecting that the claims manager stop what he is doing to listen to your spiel is not likely to happen.

Here are a couple of observations that I've made regarding marketing to claims managers:

1. Never market to these guys without the blessing of their most trusted field adjusters. The field adjusters I've found as a rule don't like it when some restorer cuts in line to visit their boss. By doing so you are in essence telling the claims manager that you are better than the restoration operators that his field adjusters are currently working with. So imagine if you will how you would feel if you were a field adjuster and had an existing relationship with a restoration company then get a call from your manager asking you why you haven't referred company "X" to any loses?
2. Before ever approaching a claims manager you must ensure that your company has built its name enough that the claims manager will recognize it when you meet with him. If they have seen a couple of your well-written estimates and one or two of their field adjusters have talked you up, then you are ready to pay them a visit. When pos-sible, have one of the field adjusters who you work with broker the claims manager visit. It's not at all complicated, it just takes a bit of finesse. After you have completed one or two jobs for a particular adjuster simply ask him if he wouldn't mind introduc-ing you to his claims manager.

Before visiting the claims manager you must be very clear on what it is you want to convey to him during your visit. Once again this is why the adjuster visits are so critical prior to meeting the claims manager. From visiting and working with adjusters you'll learn what their daily problems are and can then tailor your meeting with their manager to be the best that it can be playing off of the needs of the field adjusters. Again a field adjuster is perfectly positioned to tell you what the claims managers are looking for—after all they hear about it on a daily basis.

When I first began marketing to claims managers I would just walk in, sometimes unannounced looking like a drunken sailor in Tijuana looking for the nearest bar. I'd ask to speak with the claims manger. In my areas these people are sometimes referred to as the "Fire Manager". At any rate, when I would walk in I was usually met with that "who the heck are you look" by a manager who, while trying to be cordial, was totally confused why this stranger (being me) would waltz into his office thinking that I had something that would be of value to them. On one particular visit the "Fire Manager" came right out said: "Look, I'm a claims manager, not an adjuster. If you want to pick up work from our company it's the claims adjuster that you must get to know, not me."

First time cold call to a Claims Manager that you have never met with before and where you got his name from an adjuster:

Purpose: The purpose of this call is to introduce yourself and to ask the Claims Manager for permission to send one of your informational packets.

When: For newer restoration services this call should be made after you have completed at least three restoration projects for the insurer that the claims manager works for. For established restoration companies this call is good at any time so long as the adjusters with the company are familiar with your service and have put in a good word for your company.

Note: I'll spare the reader from having to mull through another of my long analogies of dating and the like, but would just mention that like every other relationship you'll build with those in the insurance industry it is important that you do so with a planned approach, and understand that relationship building takes a little time.

Restorer: "Good morning (claims manager's first name), this is (your name), with (your company). Did I catch you at a good time?"

Claim Manager - CM: "It's fine, what can I do for you?"

Restorer: "(CM first name), I got your name from (adjuster familiar with your work for this insurer) I'm not sure if you have ever heard of my company before?" (casually mentioning that an adjuster gave you their name will make you appear more creditable).

CM: *"Yes, I've heard of your company before/or no I don't believe I am familiar with your company."*

Restorer: "(CM name), the purpose for my call is simply to introduce myself and to ask if I would be alright to send you one of our informational packets?"

CM: *"At this point he will likely say sure go ahead and send me one, I'll take a look at it when I get the chance. In rare cases he would reply with, no don't send me one."*

Restorer: "Great! I'll drop one in the mail tomorrow. If you have any questions please don't hesitate to call."

CM: *"Okay, I'll be looking for the packet."*

Restorer: "It was great talking to you (CM name). Have a fabulous day!'

CM: *"Bye"*

Packet follow up call:

Purpose: The purpose of this call is to find out if the CM has received your information packet, and to find out if he has reviewed the materials in your packet.

When: This call is made five working days after he has received your information packet.

Restorer: "Good morning (CM first name), this is (your name), with (your company). How are you doing?"

CM: *"Okay, how are you?"*

Restorer: "Everything is absolutely great! (CM name). The reason for the call this morning/afternoon (CM name), is to see if you have had an opportunity to review the information packet we sent you on (date packet was sent)? And to ask if you have any questions about our services that I might answer for you?" (This is the part where you want to gauge what type of interest the claims manager has in your service. If the informational packet was complete he should be ready to ask you a question or two).

CM: *"Yes, I did glance through the materials. I may have an interest in meeting with you to find out a little more about your company."* At this point he will likely ask a question about one of the pieces in your packet that happen to appeal to one of his Buying Triggers or "Hot Buttons". *(Listen closely to what it is he is asking, and then give him the answer).*

Restorer: "(CM name), we really would love the opportunity to demonstrate to you how different we really are from other restoration firms. I'd very much like to meet with you for a few minutes as well, simply to introduce myself." At this point you should get a good idea if the CM would like to meet you in person. If this is the case simply ask him what day and time would be good to drop bye.

CM: *"Okay, I'll keep you in mind."*

Restorer: "(CM name), we would appreciate that!"

CM: *"Bye."*

Once this call has been made and regardless of whether or not he is willing to meet at this time, you are perfectly positioned to continue to build on this relationship. Once this guy knows your name you must not ever let him forget it!

Public Adjusters:

The following definition is from Wikipedia online dictionary:

A public adjuster is an advocate for the policyholder in negotiating an insurance claim. Public Adjusters exist because of the inherent conflict of interest that exists when one person or entity attempts to represent two sides of a financial transaction. Public adjusters are the only type of claims adjuster that can legally represent the rights of an insured during an insurance claim settlement.

There are three classes of insurance adjusters: staff adjusters (employed by an insurance company or self-insured entity), independent adjusters (independent contractors; not insurance company employees) and public adjusters (employed by the policyholder). "Company" or "independent" adjusters can only legally represent the rights of an insurance company.

Among other things, it is the public adjuster's responsibility to:

1. Investigate all coverages that may be applicable to an insurance claim;
2. Determine the appropriate values for settling all covered damages;
3. And then negotiate a settlement with the insurance company on behalf of an insured.

Typically, most public adjusters are compensated based on a percentage of the total settlement they negotiate, which negotiated settlement should always show a net gain to the insured over and above what the insurance company would have offered had it not been for the public adjuster. Thus, through such a negotiation, the public adjuster's fee is justified. Public adjusters regularly succeed in negotiating for more settlement money than insurance companies usually initially offer, because insurance companies are often intent on settling claims based on what they would pay their preferred construction or other claim vendors, not based on what the entity or location from which an insured chooses to have the affected property repaired or replaced.

However, the insured has the right to choose the repair entity, and so the public adjuster maintains this and other rights of insured's and in the process is able to negotiate a better settlement.

A large majority of policyholders are unaware that public adjusters even exist as an option to dealing directly with the insurance company representatives. A professional, conscientious public adjuster can make a tremendous difference in the amount of a policyholder's settlement.

I wasn't in the business for six months when I was informed by a colleague that marketing to, or working with a PA as they are commonly known, is the fastest way to get blacklisted by the insurers and their adjusters. I've asked adjusters the question many times of what they would think of a restoration contractor that worked with a PA and oddly enough, I got the same response as was given to me by my colleague so many years before. When reading the definition above one would assume that the PA offers a valuable service to the insured, and as a restorer on the surface it would appear that a working relationship with a PA would have the potential to be mutually beneficial for all partied involved with the exception of course of the insurer who would likely end up paying out more on the claim after a lengthy court battle.

I must withhold judgment on marketing to the PA as I honestly have no experience in working with this group of adjusters. I'm not even sure that there are any PA's in my area. If there are they have never showed in our researching.

I have only had one encounter with a PA and it went like this: In the middle part of 2004 I was contacted by a national insurer through their local field adjuster to view a water damaged property for the purpose of writing an estimate for drying services along with a detailed repair estimate. The buildings damaged by a major water loss were part of a major apartment complex.

Approximately six of the two-bedroom units in two of the buildings had suffered a large water occurrence due to broken water lines. At the time the field adjuster informed me that I would likely not be doing any drying as the loss had occurred almost three months before.

He informed me that he needed an estimate for what it would have likely cost had a "professional" been called in to dry the structure within a reasonable period of time. He also wanted the repair estimate to reflect what it would have cost to repair the damage associated with the original loss assuming that the collateral damage would be typical of this type and size of loss. By the time that I arrived to view the property it had become a severely engulfed in mold and was still testing "wet" in most areas.

The drying estimate that I wrote ended up being somewhere in the neighborhood of $19,000. The repair estimate that I submitted ended up being somewhere in the neighborhood of $115,000. So anyway, I never heard a peep from anyone regarding my estimates until in mid-2007 when I got called to testify as an expert witness for the insurer. The property owners had called in their public adjuster who also wrote his own estimates for drying as well as for the rebuild of the damaged units. This case ended up going to court for a claim of over a half of million by the property owners against the insurer. The PA's estimate was in excess of half-a-million dollars. In his affidavit he made a point to attempt to discredit my estimate even going as far as to state that the building couldn't have been properly dried and that the mold would have happened regardless of if a professional was contracted at the onset of the water loss. The apartment managers attempted to dry the six units with a total of six air movers. No dehumidification, no training, just six fans and two maintenance men manipulating an inoperable HVAC system.

The jury ruled in favor of the defendant, the insurer in this case. In my opinion this PA grossly exaggerated the true extent of damages and wrote an estimate that was baseless in void of fact.

So, I in closing this section, I'd just say that while it is nice to think that there may be these folks out there like PA's looking out for the well-being of the insured's, similar to Robin Hood taking from the rich (insurers) and giving to the poor (insured) I know at least based on the experience I just shared, I'd look long and hard at the individual PA and his credentials before jumping in blindly.

Marketing Event

When your company has grown to the point of having a significant number of contacts and connections in the insurance industry, it might be worth your consideration to host an event (in this case, a golf tournament) to network and show appreciation for the business they send your direction. The basics of this demonstration can be applied to any other kind of event you wish to put on.

Procedure: Golf Tournament

Purpose: To show appreciation for the insurance industry and increase the likelihood that they will refer work to us.

Overview: Hosting a golf tournament will get the agents and adjusters out of their office to get to know you in a fun, lighthearted setting. You want to build lasting relationships with the insurance industry. This tournament will allow them to see you in a different light. You will no longer be the annoying person who stops by their office once a month.

Steps:

Planning a golf tournament:

Four months prior to event:

1. Choose a month you want to have your tournament held.
2. Call all local country clubs that you would be willing to have host your tournament. Find out what they would charge, what dates they have available, and what they have to offer—lunch (if not, will they let you bring in a caterer), golf pro, carts, sound systems, what days they have available in your desired month, etc.
3. Decide on your location.
4. Choose a charity you would like to receive the tournament proceeds. This will help you get better attendance, sponsors, and the use of public service announce-

ments. You will want to contact the charity to get approval and make sure that they are on board with your event.

5. Create a list of people to invite to play. This list can include anyone you would want to be a sponsor of the event.

6. Decide on a cost for hole sponsorships. You will want eighteen hole sponsors. This will help with the cost of the tournament. For the sponsorship, they will be able to put a sign at the beginning of each hole.

7. Decide on a menu. You will want to keep your costs as minimal as possible to ensure you cover your costs.

8. Call to get donations for beverages such as beer, soda, and water.

9. Arrange to get some volunteers to help the day of the tournament. You can utilize your hole sponsors to allow them to each have one volunteer with their company shirt on to help.

10. Gather donated prizes to give away as door prizes.

11. You will need to decide how much the winning three teams will receive as a prize. The prizes will be for first, second and third places. You can always have a prize for the team that comes in last. It is a fun prize that everyone can joke about.

12. Figure up all your costs: food, hole sponsor signs, golf course and carts, drinks, prizes, invitations, advertising.

13. Take your total costs and subtract the money you will receive for eighteen hole sponsors. Then divide the left over cost by eighteen teams. This will let you know how much you need to charge per team. This will not include any profit for donation. You will want to charge at least $100 more per team to be able to donate $1,800. You do not want to charge any less than $75 per person or $300 per team, no matter what your costs are. This is the least amount a golfer will expect to pay to play at a charity tournament. You will want to give the most back to the charity as possible.

Three months prior to event:

14. Create your invitations; these do not have to be expensively done. Be sure to include as much information as possible on the invitation. Always include a registration form.

15. If you can get a good price, it is nice to have gifts for the golfers; balls, can/bottle warmers, towels, etc.

16. Continue to get hole sponsors and donated door prizes.

Two months prior to event:

17. Send out invitations.
18. Continue to get hole sponsors and donated door prizes.
19. Confirm details with country club.
20. Confirm details with caterer if different from country club.

One month prior to event:

21. Confirm with volunteers.
22. Start getting hole sponsor signs made.
23. Continue to get hole sponsors and donated door prizes.
24. Create list of players and teams for the day of registration.
25. Confirm order of golfer gifts.
26. Confirm drinks.

One week prior to event:

27. All player registration forms due. Finalize registration materials for day of.
28. Get all final hole sponsors signs made and picked up.
29. Confirm everything with country club.
30. Confirm everything with caterer if different than country club.
31. Confirm drinks.
32. Confirm volunteers and set up time for them to arrive and what duties they will be responsible for.
33. Check weather report.

One day before event:

34. Have all items needed ready to be packed up and taken to country club.

Day of:

35. Arrive early to get everything set up for registration.
36. Get all hole sponsors signs put at each hole.
37. Get volunteers lined up with their duties.
38. Ensure all details are arranged and moving forward as needed.
39. Eat, golf and be merry!

Your networking group will consist of companies that your restoration company does business with:

- Floor covering retailer
- HVAC Cleaner
- Plumbers
- Electricians
- Carpenters
- Lumber yards
- Job site trash container company
- Garment restoration company

These folks understand that much of your work is generated through the insurance industry and will be more than happy to help you keep getting more work since you are in turn sending them work.

Script for calling members of your networking group to ask for sponsorships:

Restorer: "Good morning (business owner name), this is (your name and company) did I catch you at a good time?"

Network Member: "How are you doing?"

Restorer: "Fabulous! Speaking of fabulous, the reason for the call this morning was to let you know that our company is hosting a golf tournament for insurance agents and adjusters on (date and time) at the (name of golf club). As you can imagine we are very excited about this outing."

Network Member: "I bet, it sounds like it is going to be a lot of fun."

Restorer: "Oh yes, it will definitely be a fun-filled day. Since most of the work our company refers to you thorough (type of service or goods. Example floor covering), we were hoping that you might want to get involved in the outing. We are looking for hole sponsors, volunteers, etc."

Network Member: "Let me think about it for a bit okay?"

Restorer: "Sure, (network member name), I'll give you a call back in a week or so to check in with you. Just keep in mind that this group is perfectly positioned to continue to send both of our company's work."

Note: I personally do not golf. However, I have for a fact sponsored many golf outings over the years. When someone from my network group asks me to sponsor an event I usually do. I expect the same of them when I call on them for support. This is what networking is all about.

Many restorers are missing out on a huge opportunity to build their business through networking with other businesses. Just think for a moment of all the different businesses that you do business with on a daily basis. Your bank, accountant, suppliers, subcontractors, auto dealerships, quick lubes, dry cleaners, gas stations, floor covering retailers, and on and on.

Now if you let these like-minded business owners know that you also like getting business back, you'll be surprised what will happen. One of the first things we do as a business when beginning a relationship with other businesses is to explain to them that we are very happy in helping their business grow, be it through referrals from us, or as is often the case our buying materials or labor from them. We expect the same in return. As cleaners and restorers most of us are in hundreds if not thousands of properties each year that can add up to a lot of revenues for those who we refer. The only problem is that it won't happen if you don't ask.

The Marketing Plan

T he following sections contain all of the components you will need to build a successful agents and adjusters referral marketing plan. As you will notice, we employ several strategies that most service companies overlook or never thought existed. To order ShowMe Marketing Solutions comprehensive manual for Marketing to Agents and Adjusters; visit howmemarketingsolutions.com

The Key to a Successful Advertising and Promotional Plan

A successful marketing and sales campaign will require several elements, each of which focuses on shifting the paradigm in the way that your company is positioned.

Advertising plays an important role in successful business ventures. It entails identifying and selecting the media that provides the greatest amount of exposure for your business and developing effective, appropriate materials for each of the media outlets. It is much more than simply running an ad in the local newspaper or on the radio or hanging a banner outside your location. This is not going to bring in the number of buying customers you need to keep your business afloat. You need to have a coordinated effort to get your name out there, thought well of, and keep it on the top of every consumers mind. You need to develop literature to go along with your advertisements so customers can take it with them and keep it in front of them. Ads are only seen a percentage of the time by a percentage of the people. Get something in front of them so they will consistently see your message and what you stand for.

Advertising keeps your services in the public eye by creating awareness. You have to do this consistently and frequently to gain "Top of Mind Awareness" or TOMA. This is a concept of being the first company consumers think of when hearing about disaster restoration or carpet cleaning. If you can achieve this, you will do well. You will be the first company that pops into their mind when needing your services. This is exactly what you want your customers to do!

When developing your advertising strategy for your service company, review your materials carefully and consider contracting outside help in designing your advertising pieces if need be. This is obviously more expensive than designing your own. However, unless you or one of your staff members are creative and skilled at graphics artwork and creative copy then the end result may be that your materials look amateurish. Use caution when purchasing materials designed by professional design houses that the pieces are tailored to the specific demographic in your region. This means, if you are in the Midwest, you do not want to have materials with pictures of homes on the ocean being worked on. These pieces will not be as effective for you as they would be for a company like yours on the coast.

Once you are satisfied with your advertising materials, select the media that will work best for your business. Advertising can be costly, so do your research and don't make rash decisions. Try to use medias that are cost effective, yet will effectively market your business for you. You may find that radio and television advertising are completely beyond your budget. Then, of course, you will have to consider print advertising to get your message across. There are many companies that offer advertising in each media category. Shop around. This will give you the best deal. Always try to negotiate the price too. Oftentimes media sales personnel will work with you on a price just to get the sale. Take advantage of this! In a later chapter I'll show you how to choose a printing company.

There are less expensive ways to advertise your company as well. These other forms need to be used in conjunction with your other methods. You will need to get yourself and your other employees business cards. These should be colorful and easy to read. If you cannot afford full color cards, definitely consider having spot color. It will appeal to the eye and differentiate your card from the many others people have. You must have business cards! This is how people will get in touch with you at a later date. Be sure you have your business name, your name, address, phone number, fax number, email address and website. You can even include a brief tag line to describe your business.

You can also place classified ads in the newspaper. If someone is looking for your services, they can go to the classifieds to find your information. Direct mail can also be a good way to introduce new services, sales, etc. Phone book advertising is expensive and usually does not yield the desired results from the investment. This does not mean to steer clear of the phone book, but be aware of the costs. You do not have to have the biggest and most colorful ad to get the most calls.

Promotional Strategies

Now we will discuss promotional strategies. Promotions entail more than just selecting the media format to market your business. It includes community involvement. This involvement can be great for your business. Your approach to promoting your business should encompass more than creating a sense of awareness about your business. It should include a commitment to your community. Giving something back is a great way to improve your company image.

An excellent way to foster this type of involvement is to meet with community leaders to find out how you can help and what events are forthcoming that could require your assistance. Keep in mind that community leaders can be an excellent networking tool especially if they feel you are genuine in your involvement. It is easy to tell the difference between those who truly care and those who are there to gain business. You can search online for a charity or look in your local phone book. There are so many to choose from, such as American Cancer Society, Hospice, Habitat for Humanity, American Heart Association and more. Pick one that you truly believe in and you will have no problem gaining from your involvement. Contact the ones you are interested in and see how they need help from the community and you will discover one you can impact the most due to their needs.

Other forms of promotion you can use would be the following:

- Employee shirts, hats, jackets, sweatshirts, etc. with your logo and company name on them. These are great to have and employees love to wear them. You can even give them to your business acquaintances so they can promote your business too. Give them away in a drawing to expand your reach.
- Pens, cups, mugs, note pads, etc. with your company information, logo, etc. You can give these away to all of your customers, those that come to your educational seminars, trade shows, etc. The possibilities are almost endless.
- Door prizes at trade shows and even in your lobby area. Give away a free room worth of carpet cleaning once a month. This will potentially bring in new business as well as getting current customers to sign up and come back in.

It is not expected or feasible to be involved in every event possible in your community and to have everything to give out to current and potential customers. This just cannot happen. I would recommend being involved in at least two different charities or organizations in your community. You will be able to see the benefit and determine the amount of time, if any, you have to put towards other activities. This image you will be creating for yourself through your community involvement efforts should be seen in your promotional materials. You want to promote the fact that you are doing great things for the community. This is all part of your public relations campaign.

Advertising & Public Relations

The way in which you advertise and promote your business will contribute to your success or your ultimate failure. Having a service and not promoting it is akin to having no business at all. As hard as this may be to believe, many carpet-cleaning operators wrongfully believe that the name of the business on the side of their van is all they need. The business, they believe, will somehow magically promote itself. As a result of this wrongful thinking they channel money that should be earmarked for advertising and promotions into items like equipment. Advertising and promotion are the lifelines of your business.

Not every company will have the same advertising budget and there are no hard fast rules when it comes to establishing your advertising budget. An initial budget for a startup cleaning business can be as much as ten percent of projected sales, while others may be as low as three percent of sales.

One of the most effective ways in which to grow any business is through the use of press releases. A Press Release is an informational piece that is typically published in newspapers. Newspapers will almost always have a section that is reserved for the local community.

The Media Kit

Before beginning the process of submitting regular press releases to the local news outlets it is important that you first develop a media kit. A media kit is an outline about your company and the services and expertise that you provide.

Your media kit should have professional look and feel about it. Remember you want to make a great first impression so do it right. I would suggest that you purchase high quality folders for your kit and use only high quality paper.

Your media kit will be hand delivered to all of the media outlets that serve your market area. These outlets will include radio stations, newspapers, Chambers of Commerce, and business associations. To gather contact information for each of these outlets you need to make a telephone call to determine who the person is who is responsible for collecting and maintaining media kits. You might also want to check with your local Chamber of Commerce as they will likely have a listing with appropriate contact persons already made up and free of charge for the asking. Once this has been determined you will compile a list with names, telephone numbers, fax numbers, e-mail addresses and position titles. This information is then stored in your office under the file heading of media contacts. Anytime you run across a story that is newsworthy, or when you are ready to submit a press release, you simply pull the file and send your chosen contacts the information release.

A few items that should be included in your media kit:

Photos - If you have professional photos of key personnel or products include them in your media kit. Be sure the photo includes all the necessary contact information. If that information is missing, create labels to stick on the back.

The label should include:

• Name and title of the person or the name of the product
• Your company name
• Company contact person and his or her phone number
• Brief caption describing the subject of the photo

Interview - Consider including an interview with one of the key persons in your organization. It could be the president, marketing rep, or another member of management that possesses skills or information that the media outlet can use. Some print journalists rework media kit interviews or combine them with a phone interview for a feature article. If you take the interview route be careful with your choice of words, and steer clear of using acronyms. Use language that is understandable and relevant to the layperson.

Newsletter, Article or Essay - If you have a newsletter, written articles, or essays relevant to your industry, you may want to include copies in your media kit. Provide information on obtaining reprints or permission to reuse the article, so the person reading the article knows who to contact.

Public Service Announcement - A Public Service Announcement (PSA) is a variation of a press release that is written specifically for radio. PSAs are particularly helpful if you're trying to call attention to an event or a time-sensitive community project. An example might be that your company is doing some charity work for the local Ronald

McDonald house and you could use some extra help in your effort. You might write a short PSA to submit to your local radio stations.

PSA Example: This PSA brought to you by ACME Cleaning

KOMU Radio FM

Attention: Brad Clinger/Station Manager

PSA: 60 words

Reference - Ronald McDonald House annual clean-up for kids program

PSA: Our community is blessed with some of the finest people and caring agencies in the state. One such agency that helps countless families each and every year now needs your help. Our local Ronald McDonald House needs your help with its anual clean up for kids. It's individuals like you that make the difference in the lives of others. Contact Bill Smith at 000/123-4567 to volunteer.

When composing your PSA keep in mind that every word takes one second to read aloud. For example, the 60-word example above will be 60 seconds on-air. Always list the number of words in the upper-left corner of the PSA, and try to keep the announcement short. Keep in mind that radio stations shy away from running any PSA that reeks, even in the slightest manner of advertising. It's acceptable to say for example this PSA brought to you by ACME Cleaning. However, saying this PSA brought to you by ACME Cleaning, Podunk's favorite and best priced carpet cleaning company is not acceptable and could possibly ruin any future chance you have with getting local radio stations to run your PSAs.

Press Releases

According to *The American Heritage® Dictionary of the English Language, Fourth Edition*, a press release is an announcement of an event, performance, or other newsworthy item that is issued to the press.

Press Releases are one of the most effective ways to build a cleaning and restoration business, yet this method is the most often overlooked. There are three primary reasons that business owners don't write press releases on a regular basis.

Reason number one: Laziness! All right, there I said it. Drafting a well-written press release will take some time and brain activity; however, the approximately 30 minutes it takes to write a release is well worth the time and effort.

Reason number two: Business owners, especially carpet cleaning operators and yes, even some restoration owners feel as though by virtue of their trade they are not worthy of positive press. This reason causes me much concern for my colleagues. If you are ashamed of the profession you chose then how can you ever expect your employees and customers to support you?

Reason number three: Many business owners do not write press releases on a regular basis because they are unsure of how to compose a well-written press release and how the process works. If this description fits you, then relax as help has arrived.

Advantages of implementing a regular press release program into your business:

• They are absolutely FREE!

That's right they are FREE. Actually, the truth is that you get paid for press releases. When you realize the tens of thousands of dollars it would cost to promote your name in the community with traditional advertising compared to the free press you quickly realize the financial benefit to your company.

• They help build your brand!

Branding

So what is a brand? *The Dictionary of Business and Management* defines a brand as: "A name, sign or symbol used to identify items or services of the seller(s) and to differentiate them from goods of competitors."

Once you have clearly identified some of the key attributes that differentiate your company from your competitors the press release will be used to convey these differences to the community on a regular basis. I'll share an example of brand differentiation and how a planned approach to using press releases can build upon your brand.

Let's assume for a moment that your carpet cleaning company is in a market where you have 15 strong competitors. All things being equal, let's also assume for discussion purposes that each of your competitors are decent companies and each are capable of delivering about the same level of service as your own company.

Now, let's also assume that you have decided to make the subject of improved indoor air quality the number one "key factor" that differentiates your company from all of the others. You have read Dr. Michael Berry's informative book, *Protecting the Built Environment; Cleaning for Health* and you fully understand the health benefits associated with clean carpet. You understand society's need for improved indoor air quality and better health. You mention your company's ability to improve indoor air quality in all of your advertising and promotional pieces.

Here's where the timed press releases assist you in building momentum in your brand differentiation. You submit regular press releases to your local media outlets. In each of your press releases you tie in the healthier indoor air quality and improved health aspect that your service offers. Even if you were to run a release about an employee who just attended an industry event you must ensure that your firm's commitment to cleaner healthier living is noted in the press release.

On the following pages are examples of three press releases. Note how the press releases serve to reinforce ACME'S Healthy Home Brand. Take note how each of the releases clearly demonstrate that ACME is all about a healthier home or office.

One of the main things to remember is that for the program to work effectively it must be done on a regular basis. One person in the company should be assigned to the position of press release writer. Many larger firms will assign the tasks to the marketing representative or in some cases an individual who is assigned to the position of public relations specialist.

For our own company we have found that one press release per month maintains our brand.

PRESS RELEASE

ACME Cleaning 1221 Your Town 000/123-4567

For Immediate Release

Date: Monday, October 23, 2006
Contact: Bill Smith/President
Phone: 000/123-4567
Fax: 000/123-7654

Contact Information

Jones Joins ACME Cleaning

Program Title

ACME Cleaning is pleased to announce that John Jones has joined the company and will serve as front line customer service representative.

"Mr. Jones has more than four years of customer service experience working in both the retail and service sector of the community. John will implement and maintain our proprietary Healthy Home Program in each of the markets we serve", says President Bill Smith.

Since joining the firm Mr. Jones has completed his carpet cleaning training and has been certified by the Institute of Inspection Cleaning and Restoration as a carpet cleaning technician. In addiiton John has completed the company's rigorous Health Home program.

Mr. Jones is a member of Toastmasters #503 and serves on the membership committee of the Podunk Area Chamger of Commerce. John is married and has two children. The family resides in Podunk.

A picture of Mr. Jones is attached.

Community involvement

This is your brand builder. It's sincere and gives the reader the clear imporession that your firm takes cleaning and indoor air quality issues seriously.

PRESS RELEASE

ACME
1221 Creek Trail Drive
Your Town
000/123-4567

—— Contact Information

March 17, 2006

FOR IMMEDIATE RELEASE

—— Program Title

Jones Attends Las Vegas Trade Show

John Jones of ACME CarpetCleaning recently attended Connections Las Vegas, the premier trade show and convention of the cleaning and restoration industry. While at the convention, Jones attended several classes and break-out sessions ranging from such topics as improving customer service to techniques for improving indoor air quality through the use of planned maintenancd.

"Indoor qir quality issues have played a significant role int he current direction our industry is headed.We believe that in the upcoming years the vital rolse that professional carpet cleaning serves in improvingt the indoor air quyality of the built environment will serve as the cornerstone to undcetstanding the necessity of maintaining a cleaner and healthire home and office, for all occupants", said Bill Smith, president of ACME Cleaning.

Jones is certified by the Institute of Inspection Cleansing and Restoration in the fields of water damage restoration and carpet and uohilstergt cleaning. He is a graduate of ACME's Cleaning for a Healthy Home, a proprietary programw hich was developed by the firm in 2002 to address indoor air quality issues.

A picture of Mr. Jones is attached.

—— Course Topic

This is your brand builder. It's sincere and gives the reader the clear imporession that your firm takes cleaning and indoor air quality issues seriously.

PRESS RELEASE

(Your Business Name & Address)

(000-000-0000)
For Immediate Release
Date: (Month/Date/Year)
Contact: (Owner/Marketing Rep.)
Phone: (000-000-0000)
Fax: (000-000-0000)
Email (abcrestoration.com)

(**Owner or Marketing Rep's Name**) of (**Your Town**) is pleased to announce the introduction of the company's "Got A Leak Program™."

The "Got A Leak Program™" was specifically designed to enhance the service experience associated with plumbing repairs and the follow-up cleaning & drying services for residential and commercial property owners, as well as to reduce the overall repair cost by providing a system of responsive service calls.

Our firm is a (**full service or specialty drying company**) that responds to (**hundreds or thousands**) of water damage claims in the (**Your Service Area**) annually. We know from experience that the longer unwanted water is allowed to remain in the structure, the more likely it is that severe damage will occur, which ultimately leads to significantly higher repair costs, said (**Owner/Marketing Rep Name**).

(**Your Company**), in conjunction with the "Got A Leak Program™" developed a one-stop call experience for those in the community who may have the misfortune of experiencing a water damage event, or for those needing the services of high quality plumbing repair. Our plumbing network system provides local plumber referrals free of charge to the community. All plumbinng contractorsa listed in the program have met or exceeded exact qualifications which include availability, experience, and dedication to high quality customer service.

(**Owner's Name**) has been involved inthe cleaning & restoration business since (**Year Formed**).

For more information regarding the "Got A Leak Program™" you may visit the company's website at www.(**Your Website Address**) or by calling (**Your Business Numer**).

Attached/Enclosed is a Got A Leak logo and a picture of (**Owner or Marketing Rep.**)

[*Note: it always needs to be the same person who was mentioned in the press release.*]

Marketing to Plumbers

Along with insurance agents and adjusters, plumbers are another group of professionals who have access to many consumers that may be in the market for restoration and cleaning services. After all, they are responding to calls on a regular basis that involve water being in places where water is not supposed to be. That alone can be enough to keep a small restoration company busy for weeks at a time. Knowing how to connect with plumbers and get them to use your name as a suggested contractor for the consumer can be a big step in the growth of your business. Read through the following section to get a better idea of how you can work effectively together with plumbing professionals.

The Research Phase and Pre-planning

Before getting deep into the subject matter involved in marketing to plumbers it might be a good idea to take some time and learn about the plumbing industry both nationally as well as on a more localized level. Doing so will allow you to see the forest through the trees. The pre-planning phase of this program will take an experienced water damage owner about eight hours to complete, assuming that he already has a written business plan. Without a written business plan the prep time will likely be closer to eighteen hours of planning. For the new startup water damage owner we estimate the preparation time of about 36 hours. The good news is that most of the work involved in the planning phase can be done after hours in your spare time.

Getting your marketing efforts off the ground

Once you have committed to marketing to plumbers it is a good idea to lay out a plan of action. Doing this will keep the program consistent and your efforts being planned will yield greater results.

Time management plays a very important role in the success or ultimate failure of your marketing efforts. We have found that allowing a set number of hours per week to work each of our niche groups is extremely helpful. For our own business, two hours per week is just about right for working the plumber market. For others the time may be a bit more or less. This is time that is dedicated to making telephone calls to plumbers, following up on potential leads, sending postcards, thank you cards, and other miscellaneous tasks. We have found that adhering to this rigorous and structured marketing schedule yields the best results.

Research

As business owners we have all met other owners who appear to always have everything happen just right for the business. Lucky stiffs, it seems like nearly everything that they touch turns to gold. We have also met those who appear to work their butts off only to end up with the short end of the stick.

The guy who struggles from day to day is just as nice and well deserving as Mr. everything I do turns to gold. Why then the disparity? The lucky stiff isn't really lucky at all. And the chances are good that what he has, he didn't amass overnight. If you take a closer look at this lucky stiff you'll find that the biggest difference between him and Mr. 'if it weren't for bad luck, I'd have no luck at all', is simply in the way they plan for their success. There have been countless books written on the subject of business planning. I'll spare the reader a lecture on business planning but will add this; while you are writing your plan keep this in mind. <u>The more you know about yourself, your competition and the groups to which you plan to sell your services, the more likely your business will be a huge success.</u> Okay, I can't resist. I'll share an example of the importance of researching.

Fictitious Example: Let's assume for just a moment that I am Ivan Turner and I represent a magazine in your hometown titled *For Women Only*. Okay with a title like that it appears at first glance that you and I would have nothing in common right? Well if you answered yes, you are correct. We have nothing in common. So my job as a sales rep for *For Women Only* is to begin my research and find areas that perhaps can give us common ground. I study your industry and learn that the vast majority of your customers are women. Hmmm, now I'm starting to get excited because with the exception of two male roommate subscribers named Frankie and Johnny, the rest of the magazines 113,459 subscribers are females. Like a kid in a candy store I delve further into the research phase to learn more about your industry. I do a quick Google search on the cleaning and restoration industry. To my surprise I learn by reading the annual salary and market survey commissioned by an industry rag called *ICS magazine* that the typical carpet cleaning operation owner draws on average an annual salary of $46,000. Digging deeper I read on the survey reports that the top two concerns of the industry members, or at least the numbers indicated by the survey respondents, shows that marketing and employee issues are at the top of the list.

Now I have at least a basic understanding of your industry. Now I'm thinking to myself, there are at least 65 carpet cleaning and restoration companies listed in the local telephone directory.

There has to be a few that would be good candidates that could potentially be signed up as regular advertisers in *For Women Only*. I know that my next step is to further my research in an effort to separate the wheat from the chaff, the rift from the raft. I conduct some basic research by checking online with my States Attorney's office to ensure that I don't inadvertently market to what I have learned through my research is called a bait and switch artist. I check with a few of my close friends and ask them who cleans their carpets? What was your experience with this cleaning company like? Would you feel confident in referring them? My friend BoBo tells me about one company that his wife absolutely loves. He says that they are a bit on the more expensive side but the service experience is awesome.

Next, I start breaking down all 65 of these companies listed in the directory and learn that twenty of them are commercial cleaners. Well our magazine is one that caters more to the lifestyles of women, their families and the home. So, I eliminate this twenty from my list. Next, I go online and visit the websites of the remaining 45 companies. As I begin to narrow my search I keep a clear vision of our magazine's core customer. We have done extensive social demographic profiling of our readership and know the following; our typical reader is a professional married female who owns her home, has 2.5 children, owns two family cars, and has at least one pet in the home. Our profile also shows that the top three concerns of our readership are as follows in the order of importance to them; security of their family, the good health of their family, the growth of their financial portfolio.

By this point I'm becoming giddy as I continue to narrow my search. It turns out that of the 45 companies left in my search only a handful have websites and of those only five mentioned that their employees were trustworthy and that the products they cleaned with are safe for children and pets. (*Remember that our customer had indicated that security of their family, and the good health of their family were their top two concerns.*) By this point I realize that we actually serve the same client base and in fact do have much in common. This isn't to say that the others are not trustworthy or that their cleaners are unsafe. For research purposes it simply puts the top five into the top tier level as they are the closest match to the preferences of our magazine subscribers. The second level tier will also be worked at a later date through other channels.

Now it's time for me to do a little more in depth research on the top tier business owners. I've identified one whose name is James Lugnut, I've learned that his friends call him KoKo. I've seen his vehicles around town and noticed that they are all clean and display sharply designed logos. Each has a smaller set of letters on the front left wheel area with the acronym BDCC. I haven't been able to break this acronymic code just yet, but figure it will make for an interesting question once we meet in person.

Now as I am getting closer to the day in which we will meet I'm shoring up my research. When I finally get to meet this Cat, I want to make darn sure that the meeting is a memorable one.

I conduct a search on Salesgenie.com to find out about how many employees he has, what his rough gross revenues are, how long he has been in business, etc.

The time has come, I've done my research and I'm ready to fire up the marketing machine. Using a proven telephone script, I give James a call.

> *"James, hi this is Ivan Turner with* For Women Only *here in Kearney."* (Notice how I immediately identified that fact that I'm a fellow Nebraskan? Without adding an identifier, James might become paranoid and hang up on me thinking I'm a secret agent and that the nature of the call is some far-fetched governmental conspiracy) *"Did I catch you at a good time?"*

> *"James, with the exception of two slender guys with soft hands, the readers of our magazine are women. My job is to assist our customers in finding new and better ways to make their lives easier and more enriching. Being women who work, most of them don't have the time or energy after a long workday to keep up with the duties involved in maintaining a clean environment for their families, especially given that many have pets to care for as well as children."*

(Notice how I'm teasing James a bit by mentioning that our readers have kids and pets? I read on his company website that they specialize in pet urine removal and his yellow page advertisement showed a young child lying on freshly cleaned carpet indicating that he understands who his core customer is. Women with children).

> *"After some research and speaking with a close friend of mine named BoBo who says that his wife loves your cleaning service, I realized that we have a lot in common."*

"I'd like to take you to lunch to share a couple of opportunities that may be perfect for both your company as well as our magazine subscribers."

Koko agrees and a lunch appointment is set.

The lunch was scheduled so that I could learn more about James and what his dreams and aspirations are for his business. This is the needs analysis. I learned that he has a young son who he thinks the world of. He coaches his little league baseball team. He has been banned from nearly every industry bulletin board for his mischievous antics. Just like the earlier research from the ICS magazine had indicated, James too has a constant struggle in finding and keeping good help. I also learned that he has a fascination or I should say, almost an obsession with corncobs and electricity. During our lunch appointment I rarely spoke of our magazine. I wasn't at lunch that day to sell advertising space. I found him to be quite affable, though I noticed that he had a habit of shaping and reshaping the tin foil that had wrapped his burrito into the shape of a cowboy hat, similar to the way a circus clown shapes balloons. It made me smile as I realized that this guy would be the perfect candidate for placing a monthly half page full color advertisement in the magazine.

Towards the end of our lunch when we both felt more comfortable James opened up somewhat and shared a lot of his personal background with me. I had learned that he preferred to be called KoKo by his friends, and asked that I also refer to him by that name. He went on to explain how he got the name KoKo. It seems that when he was a child he had a terrible fear of clowns. KoKo explained to me that one clown in particular who was named KoKo had frightened him beyond belief. As part of his ensuing therapy he was advised to adopt the name of the clown that frightened him. According to him it took much counseling and a lot of repetitive work with his hands to overcome this fear. He informed me that the shaping and reshaping of the tin foil as he did during lunch was all part of his therapy started many years before.

After lunch my research continues. The first thing I do is fill out my profile form with the information I gleaned from James. This information is going to be used throughout our long and prosperous business relationship. The day following our lunch appointment I mail James a nice hand-written thank you card.

Back at the office I search through the subjects of interest research file that we maintain and pull a couple of interesting articles regarding coaching little league baseball. I find one in particular that I feel James can benefit from along with a couple of other contacts that I network with and send them each a copy with a short handwritten note saying something like this; *Hi James, I thought that you might find the enclosed article amusing! Talk to you later.*

So, by now the reader should have a better understanding of the importance of conducting good research prior to attempting to sell your services. Developing a method of compiling and disseminating research materials is a commitment. Once started you must not stop or you will lose any momentum that you have gained.

Remember the more you put into your initial research the easier the sale will be when it is time to ask for the sale.

Where to find plumbers

- Yellow pages
- Local chamber of commerce
- Trade associations
- Home builders association
- Friends, neighbors
- On line search engines
- Salesgenie.com
- Zip-codes.com

During the pre-planning and research phase it is important to gather as much information as possible from as many sources as possible. The local phone directory is a great starting point as well as the Internet, under the heading of plumber search. For the more advanced research we have found tools like Salesgenie.com an invaluable tool for gathering more detailed information. With this program it is possible to learn about how many employees are employed by any particular plumbing contractor, estimated gross sales volume, and number of years in business, and credit rating.

(An advantage of this type of business information database is that you can also select and print directly from the screen, saving time in mail list preparation. You can use this program for each of your targeted markets).

Salesgenie.com is a subscription-based program that runs about $150 per month with a one-year contract.

The plumbing industry, like the cleaning and restoration industry, is served by several trade magazines. Subscription is free so why not subscribe? Each of these magazines features articles of interest to the plumbers who subscribe to them. These magazines are an excellent place for you to gather useful information to share with the plumbers that you market to. It makes a great impression when you visit with a plumber and are able to bring up a subject that you read in one of the magazines. He will immediately feel as though you can relate to his job. Like our own trade magazines, the plumbing ones also conduct annual surveys of their members. Once again, this information will prove valuable in learning what issues the plumbers face, then tailoring programs to assist them in improving upon their own business.

- *Plumbing and Mechanical* – www.pmmag.com
- *Jobsite Magazine – Plumbing and Heating* – www.jobsitemagazine.com/plumbing
- *Contractor Magazine* – www.contractormag.com
- *Reeves Journal* – www.reevesjournal.com
- *Supply House Times* – www.supplyht.com
- *PM Engineer* – www.pmengineer.com

There are many ways to market to plumbers. For my own service company we do a mixture of direct mail, personal visits, and through sponsoring Customer Appreciation Days at the plumbing supply houses where they purchase supplies.

The most effective ways we have found to market to plumbers are as follow;

- Quarterly direct mail pieces
- Jumbo post cards
- Quarterly CAD at their plumbing supply houses
- Lunch visits
- Lunch and learn training programs
- Networking through their contacts home builders association

It is my opinion that the most effective method of marketing to plumbers involves a belly-to-belly approach.

Many plumbers do not have an office and work out of their service vehicles. A man attempting to schedule a lunch appointment with a plumber will find it very difficult, while a woman calling a plumber to schedule a lunch appointment will do it with ease.

Based on all the types of marketing we currently do and have done in the past, the most effective method of marketing to plumbers involves a belly-to-belly approach. I'll go a step further and state that your efforts will yield far greater results by employing an intelligent, well-spoken female to market to plumbers than that of a male. Before blasting me for this statement, let me elaborate. Most men, me included, may not listen to their wives or girlfriends with the intensity as we should. However, most men deep down inside are much more responsive to a woman's suggestion, especially when it relates to business. The plumbing industry, though largely male dominated, works for a client base that is largely female dominated and a female rep can relate better to the plumber's customer.

Marketing to plumbers is just one of many niche groups targeted to build a water damage company. Prior to implementing this program we suggest that you take some time, preferably away from the noise and the hectic hustle and bustle of running a restoration business. When you find the quiet time begin the material review by asking yourself some very important questions. The more you know about yourself, the more you will get out of this program.

- What do I want my relationships with plumbers to be based on?
- How do I want the plumbing community to view me?
- How do I want the plumbing community to view my business?
- I've tried marketing to plumbers in the past with dismal results,
- Why were my results not what I expected?
- What was I actually offering to plumbers?
- Money for referrals?
- I'm not really sure, now that I think about it. How did the plumber view me?
- Do I consider myself a great salesman for the company, or should I hire a marketing specialist?
- Do I respect the plumbing industry?

So then what is it that plumbers are looking for?

I have found that the best way to start getting plumbers referrals is to first step back and formalize a game plan. The process must begin by acknowledging that the plumbing business you wish to market to is similar to your own business in that the owner has needs, dreams, and obligations just like you do.

What are some of the needs and wants of a plumbing business owner?

- He wants to grow his business
- He wants to provide a secure, friendly working environment for his employees
- He wants to have systems in place to improve efficiency
- He wants a succession plan for the day he retires
- He wants to be liked and respected
- He wants to have the ability to earn more income
- He wants to improve his customer service
- He wants to improve his marketing

We always approach our marketing efforts based on the thought of "How Can We Serve As An Extension Of Your Customer Service Team?" Plumbers are as interested in the equipment and big truck mounts you employ, as much as you are interested in the type of joint solder they use. Stay focused on your ability to serve as an extension of their customer service team.

What do you have that can be shared with a plumber?

Think about it. You are in the service sector; the plumber is in the service sector. Have you perfected a scheduling system that has given your cleaning company a competitive advantage? Do you use a customer referral system that works well? Do you use booties when you enter a customer property to protect against damaging their floor coverings?

Why not share some of the successful tools that you use with the plumber? Putting your plan together

Once you have determined the geographical area that you intend to serve, compile a plumber's list. This list should be broken down as follows;

- Plumbers who offer 24-hour service
- Plumbers who only offer 8 a.m.-5 p.m. service
- Plumbers who offer HVAC service along with plumbing services
- Plumbers who answer telephones live

www.ingramcontent.com/pod-product-compliance
Lightning Source LLC
Chambersburg PA
CBHW052000090426
42741CB00008B/1472